"Dan Millman captures the essence of the new sports movement and makes it available to a wide popular audience. *The Inner Athlete* makes it clear that everybody is an athlete and that there is a sport for everybody."

George Leonard
Author of THE ULTIMATE ATHLETE
and THE SILENT PULSE

"Dan Millman has written a superb book . . . more than just another exercise manual. This is a well-organized, clearly-written guide for the growing numbers of people who are seeking to achieve optimal levels of health, vitality, and performance in regard to all aspects of life . . . must reading for anyone interested in preventive health, physical fitness, or human potential."

Ken Dychtwald, Ph.D.
Author of BODYMIND

"Millman's book is a solid, sensible, useful volume for those of us who are unwilling to become professional athletes but who are willing to be healthier and live longer. He understands that the mind is in the body and that the body is in the mind."

Jim Fadiman, Ph.D.
Psychologist, Lecturer
Stanford University and
California Institute of Transpersonal Psychology

THE
INNER
ATHLETE

BOOKS BY DAN MILLMAN

THE PEACEFUL WARRIOR SERIES

Way of the Peaceful Warrior
Sacred Journey of the Peaceful Warrior

GUIDEBOOKS

The Inner Athlete
No Ordinary Moments
The Life You Were Born to Live

ESPECIALLY FOR CHILDREN

Secret of the Peaceful Warrior
Quest for the Crystal Castle

THE INNER ATHLETE

Realizing Your Fullest Potential

Dan Millman

STILLPOINT PUBLISHING

STILLPOINT PUBLISHING
Building a society that honors The Earth,
Humanity, and The Sacred in All Life.

For a free catalog or ordering information, write
Stillpoint Publishing, Box 640, Walpole, NH 03608, USA
or call
1-800-847-4014 TOLL-FREE (Continental US, except NH)
1-603-756-9281 (Foreign and NH)

This book is manufactured in the United States of America.
Cover and text design by Karen Savary

Published by Stillpoint Publishing, Box 640,
Meetinghouse Road, Walpole, NH 03608

Dan Millman, *The Inner Athlete;*
Realizing Your Fullest Potential

Formerly *The Warrior Athlete*

ISBN: 0-913299-97-9

Library of Congress Cataloging in Publication Data 94-65552

1 3 5 7 9 8 6 4 2

This book is printed on acid-free recycled paper to save trees and
preserve Earth's ecology.

DEDICATION

To those who understand the Moment of Truth,
those who strive again and again
and never stop dreaming;
to those with the spirit
of the inner athlete,
whether or not they made the varsity team.

Contents

Acknowledgments

My deepest appreciation to the following people who contributed, directly or indirectly, to this book: my parents, Herman and Vivian Millman, for their love and support; my past coaches, Xavier Leonard, Ernest Contreras, and Harold Frey, who helped me more than they will ever know; my teammates, for their friendship and support; and the inner athletes, East and West, who lighted the way, and on whose shoulders I stand.

Special thanks to Alfie Kohn, author of *No Contest: The Case Against Competition*, and to "Women's Sports and Fitness" magazine for their kind permission to excerpt Dr. Kohn's work—and to John Robbins, author of *Diet for a New America*, whom I have also quoted in this book, and who has made a difference in my life.

Appreciation also to Dorothy Seymour, editor of this new edition, to Errol Sowers and Meredith Young-Sowers, and to the staff at Stillpoint Publishing, for their initiative and enthusiasm in creating this new edition.

This and every book I write reflects the love, support, and patience of my family—Joy, Sierra, and China.

Prologue: The Inner Athlete in the Arena of Daily Life

**In each of us are heroes;
speak to them and they will come forth.**

—ANONYMOUS

The announcer's voice quivers with excitement as the video begins to play: "Ladies and gentlemen, you are about to see a feat performed for the first time by David Seale—a feat requiring total concentration, daring, and coordination. What you are about to observe did not happen overnight but was the result of months of preparation. Here he goes!"

A figure appears on the screen. David looks relaxed and confident, about to begin a complex series of movements and balances. He stands momentarily poised on the brink, hesitates a moment; then, with eyes focused ahead, not looking down, his mind focused completely on the task at hand, he begins to move. His body remains relaxed as he engages the first move.

Suddenly, with a tremor, he starts to fall! Quickly, David catches himself, and without wasting a moment on anger or fear, he stands again and continues toward his goal, his face serene yet concentrated.

As he nears the goal David has another near miss but again regains his balance. He reaches out, his face beaming. After a final moment of suspense, those watching let out their breath and applaud with delight as ten-month-old David Seale, inner athlete, reaches out and grasps his mother's outstretched arms. Recorded by his father's camcorder, David has walked his first steps across the living room rug.

All of us were inner athletes in our infancy—our minds free of concern or anxiety, focused on the present moment; our bodies were relaxed, sensitive, elastic, and aligned with gravity; our emotions were free-flowing expression, uninhibited, spontaneous.

We begin life with nearly unlimited potential. Most of us, however, lose touch with our childhood aptitudes as we become burdened by limiting beliefs, begin to deny our emotions, and experience a variety of physical tensions. This book reveals a way *out* of that situation by showing us a way *in* to our fullest potential.

Within each of us is a natural athlete, waiting to be born.

Introduction

The short life of the laurel wreaths worn by the ancient Olympic champions remind us that victory is fleeting, and moments of glory quickly fade. Even those who shine in their chosen field still confront the challenges of everyday life—relationships, study, and career. What approach to training best prepares us for the emotional and psychological challenges in the arena of daily life?

There is a way of training, a method of setting priorities, in which our sport or game becomes a path to a larger goal, a doorway to personal growth, a bridge to our fullest human potential. This book will show you that bridge.

I wrote *The Inner Athlete* to share the insights generated from many years of personal training, research, observation, and training other athletes, to help illuminate the internal benefits of training and to help you realize your potential as an inner athlete no matter what your present skill level or experience. I wrote this book for you, to help you unleash your highest capacities.

Whether you are a world-class competitor, a weekend player, or a fitness enthusiast, the principles, techniques, and exercises in this book offer you a less stressful, more meaningful approach to movement that connects training to life.

Training for Life

Those who have no inner life
are prisoners of their surroundings.
            —HENRI F. AMIEL

This book serves a twofold purpose: first, to provide principles, perspectives, and practices designed to expand the scope of training inwards, and second, to help you excel in your chosen field of endeavor no matter what it is.

In the quest for excellence, it is all too easy for us to suffer from tunnel vision in which the scores, statistics, and victories become the goal of training; but if we focus too much on striving, we may forget what we're ultimately striving for—to feel good about ourselves, to experience happiness, to reach our highest human potential.

This book is not about dedicating our life to our training but about dedicating our training to our life.

Athletes—Inner and Outer

When I retired from active competition and started coaching and teaching sports, I discovered that I enjoyed teaching beginners as much as advanced gymnasts. Those on the varsity team had travelled farther along the path, but the beginners had admirable inner qualities. Many of them were accomplished in other fields: music, acting, martial arts, juggling, mime, and painting and sculpting. I noticed common threads that ran through every field of endeavor; my concept of "athlete" began to expand.

Webster's Dictionary defines an athlete as "one who engages or competes in exercises or games of physical agility, strength, endurance, etc." The arena of the *inner* athlete has far broader significance and scope. In addition to practicing physical skills, inner athletes develop mental and emotional qualities that, unlike most specialized physical skills, can apply to every aspect of their lives.

We don't usually think of musicians or artists as athletes; yet nearly all of them show the same courage, mental focus, and highly-coordinated physical skills demonstrated by those who devote the same long hours to sports training. Dancers are among the hardest-working athletes, even though they seldom engage in formal competitions.

In *The Inner Athlete* I often use examples from traditional sports, games, and such fitness endeavors as golf, tennis, running, gymnastics, martial arts, football, and basketball, but the principles in this book apply equally to any form of skill training.

Outer athletes train to become *experts* as they focus on physical skill development; *inner* athletes become *masters* as they focus equally on physical, mental, and emotional skills in order to achieve integrated inner balance. Not all inner athletes reach, or even desire, competitive glory, but the inner qualities they develop make them "winners" in everyday life.

Inner athletes recognize that their relationships, their health, their careers or forms of service, and their financial success require the same attention as their physical training; in other words, the activities of their daily life require the same commitment, diligence, and step-by-step practice to achieve mastery.

Training, Inside Out

The Inner Athlete is grounded in the principle that we are a dynamic whole greater than the sum of our parts. By integrating those parts—the body, mind, and emotions—through training, we reshape ourselves and our lives inside and out.

Training, for the inner athlete, is a metaphor and mirror of daily life; it reflects our weaknesses and our strengths; it reveals our limits and our potential. At the highest level, as we enter "the zone," the moment of truth, inner training has the power to uplift our spirits to a higher plateau by allowing us to experience life in a new way.

When I use the term *training* or *practice* I refer to an intensified quality of attention, along with a commitment to refine or improve. At the core of inner training is the commitment to use our chosen field of endeavor as a model for developing a balanced approach to life. We practice our sport, but how many of us still practice our handwriting? How often do we fully engage ourselves in each daily task, whether walking or washing the dishes, in order to live fully in the moment?

I often remind my students that the musician practices music, the athlete practices athletics; the inner athlete practices everything.

The Smaller Game and the Larger Arena

In athletics, scores, performance times, and win-loss records often serve as the primary measure of success. We may be talented at turning somersaults, hitting a ball into a hole or over a net or into the stands, throwing touchdown passes, or shooting a basketball into a hoop, but these skills benefit us little in daily life. The inner qualities we develop through those activities, however—mental focus, emotional energy, and the ability to relax the body even under stress— benefit us in daily life.

Some years ago I observed Japanese Olympic ski jumpers warming up with T'ai Chi Chuan and Aikido masters teaching golf clinics. Eastern cultures have always known that mastery of the inner self is essential for success on the physical level. We are only now coming to realize that each culture, with its own rich diversity, language, and cultural views, contributes to the well-being of the whole. The blossoms of our inner understanding are just beginning to open in the sunlight of deeper awareness. The time has come to awaken the inner athlete, the peaceful warrior, within each of us.

Dan Millman
San Rafael, California
Spring, 1994

ONE

Understanding the Larger Game

Training, the heart of the athletic experience, can be represented by a journey up a mountain path. The peak represents your highest potential. Wherever you stand on your own path, it is wise to have a clear map of the terrain ahead—a way of seeing your position relative to your goals—a view of the hurdles in your path and the effort required to reach your goals.

Realistic vision, a deep awareness of your potential in a given endeavor, enables you to choose the wisest course and to train for it. From a good beginning, all else flows.

1 *Natural Laws*

Nature's way is simple and easy,
but men prefer what is intricate and artificial.
—LAO TZU

For fifteen years I trained with great energy in the sport of gymnastics. Even though I worked hard, progress often seemed slow or random, so I set out to study the process of learning. Beginning with standard psychological theory, I read current studies of motivation, visualization, hypnosis, conditioning, and attitude training. My understanding grew, but only in bits and pieces. Extensive reading of Eastern philosophy, including perspectives of the traditions of Taoist and Zen martial arts, expanded my knowledge, but I still lacked the understanding I sought.

Eventually, I turned to my own intuition and experience for the answers I was looking for. I understood that infants learn at a remarkable pace compared to adults. I watched my little daughter, Holly, at play, to see if I could discover what qualities she possessed that most adults lacked.

One Sunday morning as I watched her play with the cat on the kitchen floor, my eyes darted from my daughter to the cat and back again, and a vision began to crystalize; an intuitive concept was forming in my mind about the development of talent—not just physical talent, but emotional and mental talent as well.

I had noticed that Holly's approach to play was as relaxed and mindless as the cat's, and I realized that the essence of talent is not so much the presence of certain qualities but rather the *absence* of mental, physical, and emotional obstructions experienced by most adults.

After that discovery I found myself taking long walks alone, observing the forces of wind and water, trees, and animals—their relationship to the earth. At first, I noticed only the obvious—that plants tend to grow toward the sun, that objects fall toward the earth, that trees bend in the wind, that rivers flow downhill.

After many such walks, nature removed her veil, and my vision cleared. I saw trees bending in the wind and understood the principle of *nonresistance*. Visualizing how gentle running water can cut through solid rock, I grasped the law of *accommodation*. Seeing how all living things thrived in moderate cycles, I was able to understand the principle of *balance*. Observing the regular passing of the seasons, each coming in its own good time, taught me the *natural order* of life.

I came to understand that socialization had alienated me (and most adults) from the natural order, characterized by free, spontaneous expression; my young daughter, however, knew no separation from *things as they are*.

Still, such insights seemed more poetical than practical, until, all in a single moment, the final piece fell into place: I was taking a warm shower, enjoying the soothing spray. My thoughts were quiet; then, out of nowhere, a realization came and left me stunned: "The laws of nature apply equally to the mind and the emotions!" This may not seem like a great realization to you, but I dropped the soap.

Realizing that nature's laws applied equally to the human psyche, inseparable from the body, made all the difference for me. My world turned upside down; no longer would I view the principles of my training as merely physical. I would see them as a *psycho*physical challenge. My perceptions of the world changed; where once I viewed the world and my body as physical things, they now danced in a realm of flowing energy, to a movement of more subtle forces. This new way of seeing reaffirmed my essential connection to the laws of nature. My inner training had begun.

All that remained was to put this understanding to use—to apply it to a new way of training — in order to reawaken my innate abilities so that the fruits of training would spill over into daily life. Training became a way of life. The game of athletics had become a perfect model for the Game of Life.

The Chinese sages, in talking about the River of Life, the delicate, ephemeral existence of the butterfly, or the sway of trees in the wind, were painting pictures, drawing metaphors that pointed to the natural laws, the source of all human wisdom. All the great teachers have pointed to the same thing: that growing personally means integrating the wisdom of our life experience with the laws of nature and the open-eyed innocence of childhood.

Pursuing a natural way of training, I sought to align myself to the following lessons and laws of nature:

Principle 1: Nonresistance

There are four ways to deal with the forces of life:

- Surrender to them fatalistically. Rocks, since they are inanimate, have little choice but to surrender passively to the natural laws.

- Ignore them, and in ignorance have accidents. Creatures who lack man's perspective are relatively helpless in their ignorance and are guided only by simple instinct.

- Resist them and create turmoil. We tend to resist or struggle with the natural flow of life. Resistance wastes energy and results in various symptoms of dis-ease.

- Use them and blend with nature. Like birds that ride the wind, fish that swim with the current, or bamboo that bends to absorb the weight of fallen snow, we can *make use* of natural forces. This is the real meaning of nonresistance. Natural law has been expressed in many ways: "Don't push the river." "Let it be." "Go with the flow." "When life gives you lemons, make lemonade." "Turn problems into opportunities and stumbling blocks into steppingstones."

Inner athletes, on days that physical progress lags behind, make the best of time by working with mental and emotional issues that arise.

Nonresistance, then, is more than dumb passivity. Flowing with the natural currents of life and making use of whatever circumstances arise requires great sensitivity and intelligence.

The priorities of the inner athlete make outer accomplishments less important than internal transformations and alignment with natural law.

Inner golfers, for example, make intuitive use of the wind, of the direction the grass grows, of the moisture in the air and the curves of the land. They make use of gravity by letting the club swing in a natural, relaxed rhythm. Inner gymnasts learn to blend with the unique forces and circumstances in their environment. Inner tennis players learn to use the texture of the court to their advantage. "Conquering" is the opposite of nonresistance; the combative mind projects its own turmoil onto the world.

In daily life, those of us who resist change also inhibit growth. Bob Dylan reminded us that those who aren't busy being born are busy dying.

What a caterpillar calls the end of the world
the master calls a butterfly.

—*RICHARD BACH*

Inner athletes have dissolved any thought of resistance. They see opponents as teachers or sparring partners who challenge them to bring out their best, and they do the same for their opponents.

Opponents' movements can be used to your advantage through nonresistance. This principle is well-known in the martial arts of Judo, T'ai chi, and Aikido. "If pushed, pull: if pulled, push." Apply softness in the face of hardness—absorbing, neutralizing, and redirecting force. Use this approach to daily life.

BLENDING
The Martial Arts Principle of No-Collision

Test 1. Stand squarely in front of a friend. Tense your body. Have the friend push you with one hand as you resist. How does that feel? What happens? You are likely to experience opposition and loss of balance or control as your friend pushes you backward.

The next time he or she pushes, take a smooth step back under control; just let your body flow backward at the same speed as your partner's push—give no resistance at all. What does this feel like? Do you feel the cooperation or harmony you have created? Since you are centered and in control, you can "allow" your partner to go where he or she "wants" to go.

Test 2. Stand with your right leg and right arm

extended toward your friend, with both feet rooted lightly to the floor. Breathe slowly in your lower abdomen; relax. Cultivate a feeling of peace and goodwill. As you maintain this spirit, have your friend come toward you rapidly from a distance of about ten feet, with the intent to grab your right arm, which is extended toward him or her at hip level.

Just as your friend is about to grab your hand, you whirl around and behind your friend by taking a smooth quick step slightly to the side and beyond your partner as he or she lunges past, grabbing for the arm that's no longer there. If you do this smoothly, facing your friend as you whirl around, you'll maintain equilibrium and control as your friend totters on the edge of balance.

Test 3. This Aikido approach can also be applied to potential verbal confrontations. On such occasions, instead of verbal tussling—trying to prove a point, win an argument, overcome another with reason— just sidestep the struggle.

Simply listen, really listen, to your opponents' points; acknowledge the value of what they are saying. Then ask gently if there isn't some validity to your view also. In this way, you can learn to blend and apply nonresistance not only to "attackers" but to all of life's little problems and difficult situations. Remember that you create the struggle in your life; you create the collisions. You can dissolve struggle through nonresistance.

Nonresistance: Psychophysical Applications

In Judo, he who thinks is immediately thrown.
Victory is assured to those who are
physically and mental ronresistant.
                              —*ROBERT LINSSEN*

Stress happens when the mind resists what is. Most of us
tend to either push or resist the river of our lives, to fight circumstance rather than make use of things *as they are.* Resistance sets up turbulence that we feel as physical, mental, and
emotional tension. Tension is a subtle pain and, like any
pain, signals that something is amiss. When you are out of
your natural pattern, you will feel this tension. By listening
to your body, you can take responsibility for the turbulence
in your life rather than blaming the circumstances or other
people for your upset.

Athletes commonly resist the natural processes by *trying.* The word "try" itself implies a weakness in the face of
challenge. The moment we try, we are already tense; trying
therefore, is a primary cause of error. In more natural actions,
we omit to try. We simply walk to the refrigerator, write a letter, or water the flowers; we don't have to try to do these
things, and we perform them easily and naturally. But when
faced with something we consider an imposing challenge—
when self-doubt arises—we begin to *try.*

When competitors feel they are under pressure and
begin to try, they often fall apart. Chuang Tzu, a Chinese
sage, observed that "when an archer is shooting for enjoyment, he has all his skill; when he shoots for a brass buckle,
he gets nervous; when he shoots for a prize of gold, he begins
to see two targets."

To illustrate the effect of trying too hard, I ask you to
imagine yourself walking across a four-inch plank of wood
that is suspended a few inches from the ground. No prob-

lem, right? Now transport that plank to a height of ten feet over a pond filled with alligators. Suddenly you begin trying harder. You feel tense. We have the same plank but *a different mental state.*

Whenever we start to *try,* we set up internal opposition to what we want to accomplish. You can measure this opposition in your own physiology; when you try to keep your arm straight, you end up tensing both the extensor muscles (triceps) and the flexor muscles (biceps); you fight yourself. Athletes who *try* to stretch can feel the muscles tensing in resistance. Dieters who *try* to diet only get stronger urges for food—or gain back what is lost. Golfers who *try* to wallop the ball only end up topping it into the rough.

Inner athletes recognize that less effort can create more results. Even while engaged in intense competition they have a sense of "letting it happen" without any sense of strain, This may seem like idealistic fantasy, but numerous descriptions of the lives and duels of martial arts masters testify to the existence of this kind of grace under pressure. The higher the stakes, the more calm, clear, and relaxed these masters became, and they were unbeatable—peaceful warriors like Morehei Uyeshiba, the founder of Aikido, who, when more than 80 years of age, could easily evade an attacker wielding a razor-sharp sword, tapping the attacker on the nose with a fan while smiling, relaxed, breathing deeply.

Dr. John Douillard, in his audio-tape program *Invincible Athletics,* explains the efficacy of using a non-stressful approach to training as opposed to indulging in chronic cycles of tear-down fatigue followed by recovery.

Inner athletes take an easy, relaxed, and naturally progressive approach while working at the top of, but within, their comfort zone. In this way, they make training a pleasure, achieving a kind of "runner's high" not just in rare peak moments, but every time they train. They avoid the internal resistance or burnout that accompanies a stressful approach to training.

If you want a child to follow you, for example take her or him lovingly by the hand and pull very smoothly, very gently. The child will flow along. If you give a sudden tug, the child will pull the other way. Our subconscious minds work the same way. And since our subconscious gives us our vital energy, it seems best, in the long run, to motivate ourselves with the carrot rather than the stick.

If you play golf, don't *try* to hit the ball, just *let* the club swing. If you're a gymnast, form the intent, then *let* the body pirouette. If you play basketball, let the ball go through the hoop. In life, form clear goals, prepare, then let things happen naturally, in their own good time.

Every bamboo shoot "knows" how to bend with the wind, but inner athletes have the insight to put up windmills. Understanding the spirit of nonresistance, you create a partnership with nature. You take the first step on the path of the inner athlete.

Principle 2: Accommodation

Life was never meant to be a struggle;
just a gentle progression from one point to another,
much like walking through a valley on a sunny day.
                    —*STUART WILDE*

Let's take a look at some key points in the process of learning:

- *Athletics, like life, develops what it demands.* Development is precisely commensurate with the demand. With no demand, there is no development; with small demand, small development; with improper demand, improper development.

- *Demand requires motive.* Without internal motivation to energize a demand, there can be no persistent response.

- *Motivation requires meaning.* The motivating factor corresponds to your values in life; it must offer an improvement or benefit that you want.

- *Demand takes the form of progressive overload.* By repeatedly and consistently asking of yourself a little more than you're comfortable with, a little more than you are capable of, you improve.

- *Progressive overload takes place in small increments within your own comfort zone.* You need to stretch your comfort zone but not ignore it. Most athletes constantly work outside that zone, and they experience extremes of fatigue, strain, and even pain. By staying within (but near the top of) one's own comfort zone, inner athletes take a little longer to improve, but they improve longer.

- *Development (through overload) requires a tolerance for failure.* Development inevitably entails a constant stream of "little failures" along the way to your ultimate goals.

- *Tolerance for failure comes from an intuitive grasp of the natural process of learning.* Unrealistic expectations mean a frustrated athlete; realism breeds patience. By understanding natural laws, you develop a realistic, light-hearted approach to temporary failures and come to see them as steppingstones to your inevitable progress.

Training develops you step by step through gradually increasing demand. If realistic and gradual demands are made on the body, the body will develop. If equally progressive demands are made on the mind and emotions, they develop in appropriate ways as well.

Within its natural capacity, the human organism *will* adapt to demands made upon it. This process of accommodation reflects a law that has allowed human beings to evolve and survive through time.

Even rocks are subject to the law of accommodation. If you grind a rock with a tool, it will gradually change its shape. But if you grind it too quickly, the rock may break. Gradual demand for change, within current capacity for change, gets the surest results. Climbing a mountain is best done in small steps. If you try to do it in huge leaps, the result may be counterproductive.

Words I've repeated to many athletes and people from all walks of life are: "Trust the process of your training; trust the process of your life." In the larger picture, there are no mistakes, only lessons. Let's learn from every challenge, every success, every failure.

Accommodation: Psychophysical Application

Many of us are so goal-oriented that we forget to enjoy the journey. I'm reminded of an ancient Chinese curse: "May you achieve all your goals." The paradox is that if we enjoy the process of striving for our goals we are more likely to reach them and to discover for ourselves that getting there is more than half the fun.

Accommodation is a law, as certain as the law of gravity. Yet most of us don't trust the law because of self-doubt or confusion. We may wonder, "Can I really become good at this?" "Will I be able to accomplish my goal?" "Will I find success?" Such questions only create tension and weaken motivation.

Instead, be resolute. Realize progress is mechanical: If you practice something over time with attention and commitment to improve, you will. Some people may have a unique combination of psychological, emotional, and genetic qualities to become world-class, but *anyone* who practices over time can become competent, even expert, in any chosen endeavor.

———— PROOF OF THE PUDDING ————

Here's a simple way to see how the law of accommodation works: Choose a physical action that is presently a little beyond your reach. It may be a push-up, a sit-up, a one-arm push-up, a handstand push-up, sitting on the floor with your legs straight out in front of you and touching your toes, running in place for five minutes without becoming tired.

Once you've chosen your feat, attempt to perform it several times in the morning and again in the evening. Do this *every day.* With each attempt, you're asking your body to change. Ask politely—don't overdo it. But be consistent.

Set *no* goals of accomplishment, no time limits, no specific number of repetitions you must do each day. (Some days you may feel like doing a little more; other days, less.)

Continue this for a month, and see what happens. Without really trying, you'll find your body complying with your "polite request."

Apply the same approach to any change you'd like to make in your life. Reaching your goal just takes a little time and persistence. The body will adapt. Trust the process; ask and it shall be given.

Applying the law of accommodation generates new levels of confidence, responsibility, and commitment; we know full well that our success depends upon the demands we are willing to make on ourselves. We also achieve a sense of clarity and inner security, because we *know* that if we decide to do something that is within our capacity, we will succeed. We don't wonder whether a rock will fall toward the ground if we drop it, so why should we doubt our eventual success?

Principle 3: Balance

Every athlete recognizes the need for balance. Yet balance is far more than a sense of equilibrium; it is a Great Principle informing every aspect of our bodies, our minds, our training, and our lives. I call this the Goldilocks principle: "Neither too much nor too little."

Inner athletes, oriented naturally toward balance, move neither too fast nor too slow, neither too far to one side nor to the other, neither too active nor too passive, too high nor too low.

Balance determines the correct pace, timing, and accuracy that athletes depend upon. The human body itself depends upon a delicate balance of blood chemistry and body temperature; it must breathe neither too fast nor too slowly; it must develop into a unit neither too fat nor too lean, neither too muscular nor too emaciated. Even our intake of water and essential nutrients must be balanced. Everywhere we look, we can see the law of balance at work.

The law of balance is the recognition of natural limitations. It is possible, of course, to go beyond the boundaries dictated by this law, just as we can temporarily resist the other natural laws, but in the long haul we pay an inevitable price: the principle of action-reaction eventually takes over; the odds are "with the house."

Applying this principle to our training, when we are in balance we become immune to impatience and frustration because we recognize that for every "up" cycle there will naturally be a "down" cycle—and vice versa. It would be wholly unrealistic to expect only "ups." ("Having it all together" is like trying to eat once and for all.)

Our progress in life tends to consist of two steps forward, then one step back. Some days are high energy days and others are not. We win some and lose some. Seeing this, even when training has its ups and downs, our mind and emotions stay in balance and our spirits remain high, buoyed by higher wisdom of the law of balance.

Balance: Psychophysical Applications

As it becomes more clear that the world—and our training—necessarily involves body, mind, and emotions, balance takes on even more profound significance, because we begin to see that physical problems are symptoms of imbalanced mental and emotional patterns. When we feel physically off, we ask, "What's going on in my mind and emotions?"

The word "centered" is a useful one to describe a state of inner as well as outer balance—to a state of simultaneous physical, mental, and emotional equanimity. In fact, the three centers are so intimately connected that an imbalance in one will affect the others. The martial artist knows that if a person is mentally distracted or emotionally upset, he or she can be pushed over very easily.

Experience the following tests in order to discover for yourself the uses—and abuses—of balance.

——————— **YOUR MIND-BODY BALANCE** ———————

Test 1. Assuming that you're relatively calm and

happy right now, stand up and balance yourself on one leg. (If that's very easy for you, do it with your eyes closed.) Make a mental note of the relative ease of this act.

Wait until the next time you feel upset—angry, sorrowful, fearful, or distracted—or you are thinking about a current difficulty in your life; then give yourself this same balance test. You'll notice that one of two things will happen: If you are "meditating on your upset," you'll lose your balance easily. If you are "meditating on your balance," you'll lose your upset. Physical balance and emotional upset are like fire and water; they don't mix well.

Test 2. We can also gain control of an imbalance in body, mind, or emotions by deliberately doing something out of balance, in order to see the imbalance clearly and to control it.

To illustrate: The next time you practice any game, spend a few minutes deliberately off-balance, then back on balance, then off balance, then on. You will see your game begin to improve afterward.

If you're too prone to act in one way, see if you can play at acting too much the other way. If, for example, you're too timid in your play, try being too aggressive. If your tennis serves veer too far to the right, make an effort to send them too far to the left.

This practice is going to feel awkward, like wearing a suit two sizes too small; nevertheless, it will do you a world of good, because when you play with both sides, you can find the middle and regain your balance. In Chapter 7 I go into more detail about this invaluable method of attaining balance.

Principle 4: Natural Order

Natural order accounts for progressive development through time. In nature, one season follows another without haste in the proper sequence. A tree grows from a seedling as an adult grows from an infant. Progressive development doesn't work backward, nor can the process be rushed; it's all clocked into the natural order of things.

Only the human being is in a hurry. Our minds race faster than life. Ignoring the law of natural order, we set time goals for ourselves, then rush to reach these arbitrary goals. It's true that we must have some goals; they're essential for movement in life. Without them, we wouldn't get out of bed in the morning. Yet we should not attempt to make rigid goals in *time*. Time goals are unrealistic, because we cannot foresee the future. The longer-range our goals are, the less realistic they will be. We can foresee the direction of our progress, but we cannot foresee the pace. Life holds too many surprising twists and turns, and it contains too many changes for us to second-guess the natural order of things.

Progress is a function of both time and intensity. You can spend less time and more intensity, or more time and less intensity. They must be balanced.

If we overtrain, we may seem to make more rapid progress, even enjoy a short time of glory, but we eventually experience a natural consequence of a life out of balance: burnout.

Whatever cycles we pass through, no matter what our pace, it's best to trust in natural order—to enjoy each day, come what may, with all the energy and humor at our command. Humor is a good sign that we have a balanced perspective. After all, no matter how magnificent our athletic aspirations or achievements, we remain eternally tiny specks in the great universe; missing a putt or double-faulting a serve is hardly going to shake up the cosmos.

Natural Order: Psychophysical Applications

Everyone of us at one time or another has probably thought, "I should be doing better—I should be achieving faster." This is often an indicator that we've forgotten the law of natural order. Like the word "try," the word "should" has little place in the mind of the natural athlete. "Should" implies a dissatisfaction with *things as they are.* It is the ultimate contradiction; it's the trembling foundation of neurosis. Your time is too valuable to spend stewing over things that are not.

Of course, whether training is too "intense" or too "easy" depends upon your capacity. As a coach, I always set up an organized program as a general framework, expecting the individual athletes under my guidance to modify it according to their differing capacities. They need to trust their inner sense more than an external program.

One good measure of our alignment with the law of natural order is our level of comfort and enjoyment during the process of training. Certainly, we have good and bad days, but in general, if we push ourselves too much too long we may lose the original sense of joy we had as beginners.

One Olympic swimmer stated publicly that she would be glad when the Olympics were over so she would never have to look at another swimming pool. Can you imagine carrying the same attitude about life? "I've achieved greatness, but I can't wait 'till it's over." As we train, so we live; as we have learned to live, so we train. By examining one, we come to understand the other.

We cannot escape the consequences of nature's laws. There are no tickets for violations, but "outlaws" from nature create their own prisons.

Balance your life between pleasure and pain. Become sensitive to the natural order of things. Practice nonresistance by making use of whatever you meet on your own path, your own journey. Follow a step-by-step process, and trust what comes. Working within natural law, you will not only find self-discovery and a measure of success, but you will enjoy life more with each passing year.

Alignment with natural laws gives us the first keys to athletic freedom. In the following chapters you will see the uses of these four great principles in transcending beliefs that limit your self-concept, in hurdling emotional blocks, and in developing inner as well as outer talent—all as preparations for your journey up the mountain path.

2 *The Power of Awareness*

Life is a Great School, and nature is the ultimate teacher, but without awareness you can't hear the teacher. Awareness transforms life's lessons into wisdom; it can translate confusing circumstances and events into useful knowledge. Awareness, then, is the beginning of all learning.

Learning is a response to a demand to grow—to do something you couldn't do before. The process of learning therefore naturally involves errors. Errors aren't the problem; ignoring or misunderstanding them *is*. In order to correct an error, you must first be *fully* aware of it; then the error is inevitably going to be corrected.

The usual way of measuring how you are progressing in your sports activity is by observing the results. In other words, if you win the match, sink the putt, accomplish your goal, then everything seems fine; but if the match is lost or the ball ends in the rough, you know *something* is wrong. Awareness can translate that "something" into specifics.

> **Most problems precisely defined
> are already partially solved.**
> —*HARRY LORAYNE*

If awareness were merely intellectual, then infants couldn't learn. There is more to awareness than conceptual understanding. Awareness represents a kind of whole-body sensitivity arrived at through direct experience. Trying to learn a skill without total awareness is like trying to apply a stamp without adhesive—it just won't stick.

In life as well as in training, errors are always with us. We can say that learning a new skill is a process of refining errors to the point where they no longer hinder a desired goal. Errors exists even in our NASA space program, but they have been minimized to an almost invisible level of tolerance. Even the "perfect 10.00" routines of Olympic gymnasts contain errors, but they are small enough to be considered irrelevant. Smaller errors make the expert.

It's desirable, of course, to be aware of strengths as well as weaknesses. Awareness of our strong points brings confidence, inspiration, motivation, and satisfaction. Only awareness of our weaknesses, however, allows us to strengthen our weak links and improve consistently.

Awareness, Disillusion, and Success

Awareness heals, but it isn't always pleasant. On the contrary, the growth of awareness can feel like a disillusioning process. During my first few months of Aikido training I became quite disillusioned. The flowing martial art of Aikido requires relaxation-in-movement even while under attack. In the face of this demand for relaxation, I began to notice a great deal of tension in my shoulders. At first I thought that Aikido was "making me" tense, but I gradually realized that I was only becoming aware, for the first time, of tension I had always carried.

Freshmen on the Stanford gymnastics team going through this process of insight, awareness, and disillusion, would sometimes feel frustrated and tell me, their coach, how they "used to be better in high school" and how they were "going downhill."

This concerned me—until I saw films of them from the year before, and it was obvious that they had improved radically. They had simply raised their standards and were more aware of errors than they were the previous year.

One sure sign of growing awareness is that you feel as if you are "getting worse." Awareness in sport, in relationships, in any learning often entails a momentary drop in self-esteem, a dent in our self-image. Because of built-in defense mechanisms, therefore, most of us have a tendency to resist awareness.

It is important to understand and account for this internal resistance to awareness so that you can avoid the discouragement and frustration that has caused some athletes to quit a sport just when they are beginning to become proficient because they imagine that they are "getting worse."

Whole-Body Awareness

Most athletes have the courage to see and overcome physical errors, so that one aspect of themselves is developed. The way of the inner athlete, however, is to increase awareness of weaknesses in body, mind, and emotions. To do so we have to be willing to lose face, to see ourselves momentarily in a light that is less flattering than we would wish. We *all* have mental and emotional as well as physical traits from childhood that are maladaptive, immature, and downright silly. In most people these traits remain hidden from their own awareness, only to surface momentarily in times of upset, pressure, or crisis. Awareness is like sunlight over a dark well. We don't see the little demons lurking there until the light of awareness shines directly overhead; then we notice all these undeveloped qualities in ourselves and gain both humility and compassion.

If we resist seeing physical weaknesses a little, we resist awareness of mental and emotional weaknesses *a lot.* There are two very good reasons for this: First, *it's easier to see physical errors.* The results are on a gross level, right in front of us. If we're missing the baseball, for example, it's pretty obvious that we're making an error. Emotional and mental weaknesses are more subtle, harder to discern. Second, *we identify more with our minds and emotions than we do with our bodies.* What we identify with, we tend to defend. We defend our self-image, our loved ones, our values much more ferociously than we defend those things we consider separate from ourselves.

I once saw in a magazine a cartoon showing a man pushing a small cart with frozen ice cream inside. He stood listening to a speaker on a platform who was sermonizing to a small crowd. The ice-cream vendor's face showed increasing interest and agreement as the speaker said, "Down with Fascism! . . . Down with Communism! . . . down with big government! Down with politicians!" Suddenly the vendor's face grew sour, and he walked off, offended, muttering under his breath. It seems the speaker had added, "Down with ice cream!"

You may doubt the fact that we identify with (and defend more intensely) our minds and emotions than our bodies, but do you notice how people feel less awkward talking about their physical illnesses than about an emotional or mental problem? If you tell an athlete he looks clumsy on a particular occasion, he might be a little upset, but if you tell him he appears to be stupid or immature (displaying mental or emotional weaknesses), he's far more likely to be upset or defensive. This defensiveness is the primary mechanism of resisting awareness of errors. The natural athlete cannot allow himself such defensiveness; it's too heavy a burden to carry if he is to become light and free.

If you are to become the natural athlete, aligned with the natural laws, you must bring nonresistance to awareness. Acuter observation will detect the weaknesses, cut through illusion, and transform your errors into whole-body awareness . . . and power. Hidden weaknesses surface in the heat of competition and training, so the athletic arena has tremendous potential for whole-body development.

In understanding our built-in tendency to resist detecting our own foibles and weaknesses, we can see why the process of learning isn't simple for adults. Children, on the other hand, as residents of an adult world, are used to losing face; making errors is a major part of their lives. Most of what infants *do* is make errors. They wet their pants, fall over, drop things. Yet they have nothing to resist, so the progression of awareness-practice-correction is natural to them. If it were so for us, learning would accelerate rapidly.

What happens to most of us in our athletic endeavors is that we're "sort of" aware of what we're doing wrong, and we "sort of" try for a while to correct it. Often, however, we feel momentarily worse when we try to make corrections based on confused awareness, so we tend to go back to whatever habit patterns we've been accustomed to.

It's often easier to stay confused. One athlete under the authoritarian rule of an abusive coach who was literally running him into the ground described to me yet another in a long line of injuries. When I asked him why he didn't find another coach, he replied with a sigh, "Well, at least I'm used to him."

In sports, relationships, and other aspects of daily life, we often get stuck in old habits for the same reason—at least we're used to them. The less flexible we are, the less willing to take risks, the more likely we are to remain stuck in old habits that no longer serve us. Sometimes it takes physical or emotional pain to generate the awareness and action necessary to change.

> *Then the time came*
> *when the risk it took*
> *to remain tight in a bud*
> *was more painful than the risk it took*
> *to blossom.*
>
> *—ANAIS NIN*

The Growth of Awareness

Awareness, like everything else, is subject to the natural laws. It happens not all at once but in a natural order, from gross to subtle. Your growth in awareness is similar to self-sculpture. First you determine the shape you want to bring out of a stone (your goal). Then you begin hacking and hewing. This "rough cutting" is your general awareness. Later you are ready for the detail work and polishing—the most subtle awareness.

An example of gross awareness is noticing that you sometimes fall down accidentally or that you tend to have an explosive temper and hit people, or that you often become distracted and forget where you are. An example of subtle awareness is the close attention that the diver pays to the position of his hands and fingers even during a triple somersault, or the control of internal organs some yogis have mastered.

A Japanese story illustrates the respect for refined awareness common in some Eastern cultures.

> An old samurai warrior knew his time on earth was near an end and wished to bequeath his sword to the brightest of his three sons. He designed a test.
>
> He had a friend hide just inside the barn, above the doorway, and gave him three bags of rice. He then invited each son inside, one at a time.
>
> The first son, after feeling the rice bag fall on his head, drew his sword and cut the bag in half before it hit the ground.
>
> The second son halved the bag even before it hit his head.
>
> The third son, sensing something amiss, declined to enter the barn—and so earned his father's sword.

We can say that beginners are those who have not refined their awareness of errors relative to a particular skill. In this sense, we are all beginners, for no matter what we've accomplished, there are always new refinements for which we haven't yet developed subtle awareness. In our journey up the mountain, we're all beginners in new territory.

The Margaret Analogy

At Oberlin College, I once had the pleasure of coaching a dedicated diver named Margaret. Her progressive growth of awareness in learning a particular dive parallels the stages we all go through in training—and in daily life.

After her first diving attempt, she had no awareness of what she had done wrong and had to rely entirely on my feedback.

After several attempts, she could tell me what she had done incorrectly after the dive was finished and the errors had been made.

Before long she was becoming aware of her errors during the dive.

Finally, in one attempt, her awareness was integrated with body, mind, and emotions *before* the dive, and the errors were corrected before they were made. The dive was beautiful.

This example has profound implications for daily life, because we go through the same process in all kinds of learning situations.

There is a great difference between recognizing an error, which comes after a simple explanation, and accepting an error as an error—an acceptance that implies full responsibility for correcting that error. Full awareness implies willingness to change, and we may not be ready to do that. An example is a young woman on a gymnastics team who was overweight. She *recognized* that she needed to lose her extra fat. She could see it in a mirror. Yet it took her one full year to become *fully aware* of this weakness as an *error*. For a long time she had resisted recognizing what was obvious to her friends—in the same way alcoholics may go for years without recognizing the obvious.

In athletics or daily life, then, a habitual error must be *felt*, not merely acknowledged verbally, before the person making that error will generate the motivational impulse to change.

I had a friend named Roger who never stopped talking; maybe he even talked in his sleep. He knew that he was a marathon talker—in fact, it was one of his favorite topics of conversation. Yet Roger did not see his habit as an *error* that was driving his friends away.

Most of Roger's acquaintances, wanting to be tolerant, never told him that he was an outright bore. One day at a party, in the middle of one of his favorite monologues, a young woman told him he was "deadly boring." She told him that it was impossible to have a dialogue with him and pointed out how people walked away as he approached.

At first Roger was very upset. He had lost face. Before long, he began to notice his talking sprees as an error— after they had ended. Within a few weeks he had begun to notice his compulsive verbalizing as he was talking. (In fact, it began to seem that his endless talk was getting worse than ever.) Eventually, Roger remembered to quell his talks before he got going. He became a good listener—and, just as in fiction, he ended up marrying the candid young woman.

As Roger learned to control his mouth, we can all learn to control our bodies. Awareness is the key, the ability to hear the lessons all around us.

Teachers who understand the progressive growth of awareness need never be impatient with their students, because a wise teacher realizes that telling students of their errors is a limited form of communication, addressed only to their minds. It takes longer for full awareness to pervade all three centers, thus giving us the emotional impulse, mental clarity, and physical ability to change.

That is how awareness grows in the diver, skier, cellist, pool shooter, golfer, potter . . . and you. Realizing the natural growth of awareness allows you to be your own gentle teacher. Give yourself sufficient time in which to learn.

Feedback Aids to Awareness

We've all run into a situation in which we know that we're making an error but don't know what it is. In situations like this, it saves time to use an aid to awareness. The following are helpful aids.

The Other Students. The errors and successes of other athletes can serve as lessons and as inspiration.

Students less skilled than you remind you of your own progress. When you observe these beginners improving just as you did, you understand that you can also continue to improve.

Students who are more advanced than you are can serve as examples to copy. Learning from example is the way infants learn—and probably the most natural way to learn. Advanced athletes can inspire you by showing that high-level skills *are* accessible to us all.

Visual Feedback. Nothing serves the growth of awareness so instantly and so well as seeing a film or videotape of your own movements. Even a mirror can help you become realistic about your strengths and weaknesses.

The Teacher. The videotape or film can show you what you look like, but only the teacher can pinpoint the specific errors you are making in order of priority. The teacher is an intelligent feedback aid who can analyze and communicate information about errors and the ways to correct them.

The teacher has journeyed further up the mountain than you have and can show you how to avoid some of the pitfalls on the path. Throughout history, the teacher has been one of the best sources of feedback in the growth of awareness.

Exaggeration. If you have no access to films or teachers or videotapes and want a shortcut to awareness, then all you have to do is *deliberately exaggerate* your errors. If you are slicing your golf ball or continually falling in one direction, do it even worse—on purpose. This serves two purposes: First, the error becomes obvious, and your awareness grows instantly. Second, your errors become conscious, deliberate, and controlled instead of unconscious. They thus become far easier to correct.

Some teachers advocate letting yourself make errors, to cultivate patience and be free from self-criticism. This technique is helpful. But in going beyond this and deliberately repeating the error consciously, you will soon find yourself free of it. *Deliberate error* is no longer an error.

3 *Preparation*

**If I had six hours to chop down a tree,
I'd spend the first four hours sharpening the axe.**

—ABRAHAM LINCOLN

Preparation is the foremost key to success. If we want to build a house, we had better prepare a strong foundation. Every step of the process is important, but if we lack a foundation, we compromise our entire structure. In order to succeed in any field, we also have to build a foundation of body, mind, and emotions.

If we don't prepare, we run the risk of developing bad or compensatory habits. And bad habits are like a tall tree or comfortable bed: easy to get into but hard to get out of. In fact, nearly every difficulty we face in our chosen form of training can be traced to skipping steps in the past—to a weakness in our foundation.

> *Champions in any field
> have made a habit
> of doing what others
> find boring or uncomfortable.*
> *—ANONYMOUS*

World-class and professional athletes regularly go back to basics and strengthen their foundation. The reason most of us experience so many difficulties in our own training is that we were never taught to build an inner foundation based on mind and emotions, we just went straight to physical skills. We therefore never learned how to learn.

The way most children learn athletics in school amounts to pure Darwinian survival. The teachers run them through their paces and, in the end, the survivors make the varsity; the others are left behind and often never discover their own potential.

Recognizing that all things in nature have a gestation period and must go through the proper stages in order to be formed, inner athletes begin with *thorough* preparation.

Complete preparation is both the most difficult and the most important part of any learning process. Ninety-five percent of making Chinese vegetables is in the preparation: heating the wok to just the right temperature, cleaning and fine-slicing the vegetables, making sure they are crisp. Then the cooking is easy.

In painting a car, you must first go through the arduous work of cleaning the body, sanding it, filling in nicks, pounding out dents, sanding again, cleaning again, masking, priming—then, swish! the painting is easy. What would the paint job look like if you didn't prepare the auto properly first? It would look like the usual athlete—both are uneven, bruised-looking, and quick to show wear and tear.

Any obstructions you have ever encountered or may someday encounter are the direct result of insufficient or improper preparation. Athletes who have developed strength but ignored the need for suppleness will tend to compensate for their lack of flexibility with more strength. The substitution may appear to work, but the resulting imbalance will, at some point, obstruct or hinder ease of learning.

Picture an iceberg floating in the sea; the visible tip represents the physical skills we demonstrate in performance or competition. The larger portion of the iceberg, under "see" level, represents your preparation. It may not be visible from the surface, but without it, the showy part would turn over and sink.

Learning is like building a house. *The skills* are the visible part of the *upper-house structure. Physical talent* makes up the foundation of the house. *Mental and emotional talent*—inner qualties like strong focus and stable motivation—are the *ground* on which the house and foundation stand.

The foundation of a house and the ground beneath the foundation aren't very flashy. No one drives by a house and says, "Wow! Will you look at that classy foundation!" But a solid foundation based upon internal preparation will give that house, and your athletic career, a long life.

One coach I'll call Ernie developed more Olympians than any other I know of. His secret was preparation: He saw to it that the young athletes under his guidance spent their first high school year working almost exclusively on the qualities that make up physical talent.

Some of his athletes found the preparation boring, and they quit. But the ones who understood the importance of preparation stuck with it and went on to became some of the finest high school athletes in America, sought after eagerly by many college coaches.

We would all like to find shortcuts up the mountain path. Consider two spaceships in a race to Mars. Spaceship A takes off first with a head start, but as a result of rushed preparations it's not fully fueled and is missing some provisions. Spaceship B remains standing until all preparations are complete, taking on a full supply of fuel. At first this spaceship seems to lag behind at first. Only one ship will make it there and back again: the spaceship that is completely prepared for the journey.

Charting a Proper Course

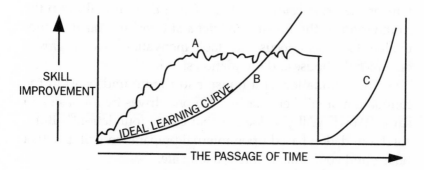

The above chart illustrates three possible learning patterns.

Curve A shows the hasty, random, up-and-down learning curve of most athletes. They improve rapidly at first, but as the skill requirements advance, weaknesses begin to have greater influence on their performance. Because of insufficient preparation—and a resulting weak foundation—the athletes' up-and-down cycles are amplified, and progress eventually levels off.

If you reach this point, you might begin to think you're "too old" for the activity or that you've "reached your potential." Motivation may wane. You may decide that "other things in life are really much more important" and eventually retire.

Curve B is the path of the total athletes. At first they appear to improve very slowly. The path is initially difficult, with little to show. These athletes are working "below the waterline," developing a hidden foundation. Gradually but surely, the learning curve begins to turn upward, until progress accelerates at a rapid, consistent, and almost effortless pace.

Curve C is really the most important, because it represents a second wind for most of us. If your preparation has been insufficient and you have been stuck on a plateau, you can duplicate the path of the natural athlete by first going back for a time—perhaps a few months—to do intense work on the "talent foundation" that will be explained fully in the following chapters and on fundamentals. Allow yourself to progress very slowly. In a relatively brief time, your progress will begin to accelerate again, and you will pass your old marks.

Step-by-Step Preparation

Whether you are concerned with physical, mental, or emotional preparation, a step-by-step approach to the task at hand can assure success. You may be trying to work out a complicated problem in physics; you may be job-hunting; you may want to do a double back somersault. Each of these tasks may seem difficult. But each can be broken down into a series of small steps that together represent a gradual methodical process leading to the final goal.

Do what you can
with what you have
where you are.
    —ANONYMOUS

As we focus our energies on each of the intermediate steps, we make the process itself much more manageable and enjoyable. Almost without noticing, we find ourselves nearer to the goal. Anything and everything in life can be broken down into its component parts, and the more adept you become at this preliminary step to accomplishment of your goal, the more you'll amaze yourself by what you can do.

The Illusion of Difficulty

"Difficulty" has no absolute meaning; it is relative only to your preparation. If you're prepared—if you've developed all the necessary physical, mental, and emotional qualities—then nothing will be difficult for you.

A common experience for many athletes is to find learning easy at first and more difficult as time passes. This increased difficulty is such a common pattern that we accept it as normal. Yet it is not the natural pattern; it is merely a reflection of insufficient preparation.

Inner athletes prepare well with a good "talent foundation," making learning easier and easier as time passes.

In order to avoid falling onto path A, we might take a look at the primary reasons people choose what looks like a shortcut:

- They might not appreciate the importance of thorough preparation.

- They might not know what thorough preparation consists of.

- They may be in a hurry, seeking shortcuts, because they lack a realistic map of understanding.

- Lacking confidence, they may avoid a path that appears slower at first and promises few immediate rewards.

- They may have a teacher who falls into one of the above categories.

Many coaches and teachers allow or even encourage the use of shortcuts in order to "keep the students interested" or because it's "more practical." Immediate competitive pressures and deadlines aggravate a tendency toward the use of shortcuts, but they are never advisable. The best teachers know that.

Beginning students cannot be expected to have a complete understanding of the training process and certain priorities within it. Therefore, an intelligent and patient teacher is one of the most important aspects of your training. Choose with great care.

Choosing a Teacher

The teacher is your guide along what might be thought of as a mountain path. Some guides are familiar with the lowlands; others can show you the entire way. The best guides have seen all their own weaknesses and therefore have insight into yours; they can show you the obstacles but also point out the interesting side roads and beautiful scenery along the way. If your guide insists that you travel exactly the same path he or she did, then that guide's knowledge is limited. Seek a guide who can assess your qualities and find the best way for you. A fine teacher filled with natural awareness can be a beacon to help light your way.

Second only to parents, teachers of movement can have a profound influence on a student's self-concept and outlook on life. A genuine teacher conveys useful lessons of living through the form of movement. An average teacher just teaches skills. Beware of knowledgeable, skillfull teachers who can develop "winning" teams but will at the same time smother the fundamental enjoyment and freedom of athletics.

If you can appreciate the importance of a good teacher, pick one for yourself or for your child with the same care you'd use to pick a surgeon. You wouldn't want to be operated on by mediocre surgeons—even if they are nice, have offices right near your house, or charge a few dollars less. Yet this is how many people pick movement teachers. Finding a superior teacher for yourself or your child is worth some research, and is money well spent, because an inspired teacher can be a positive influence that children (or adults) will remember the rest of their lives.

Teaching is an *art of communication.* If one teacher possesses 100 volts of knowledge but can effectively convey only 20 volts to his students, that teacher will be less effective than a teacher who has 50 volts of knowledge along with the ability to convey it all.

Teachers who have great competitive records with many championships may be good resources because they have traveled far, and their accomplishments may inspire their students, who are likely to listen with respect and attention and follow through with their directions. But do not be overawed by a competitive record or a whole list of advanced degrees. *The important thing is not what teachers know but what their students know, not what teachers can do but what their students can do.*

A good teacher can speak the language of the intellect— words—and communicate clearly so that the student understands.

An excellent teacher can speak the language of the body—by showing the muscles, bones, and nerves how an activity should feel if done properly.

A great teacher speaks the language of the emotions— by inspiring and motivating, and by rekindling the original love of the activity with which you began.

The master teacher can do all three.

Gifted teachers may be found in unexpected places. Remember that the best teachers not only teach a subject, they convey principles of living through a subject.

The Preparation of Children: A Note to Loving Parents

Children are likely to live up to
what we believe of them.
        —*LADY BIRD JOHNSON*

As we look around ourselves and at the haste and rushing of today's time-schedule world, we can understand why we tend to hurry now and then. Our haste to achieve spills over onto the children, and nowhere is this more apparent than in children's athletics. Perhaps before long we will see Diaper League Championships, complete with preschool cheerleaders. Instead, however, I recommend the following considerations:

Movement play for young children (and even infants) is wonderful. It stimulates them, exercises them, and opens their vital little bodies to a means of enjoying and discovering their relationship to the natural laws. Skills, however, aren't important for children. What is important is that they learn:

- to feel good about their bodies.

- to feel success in their early endeavors on the basis of beginning with relatively easy tasks.

- to learn the enjoyment of active movement that stems from accomplishment.

- to develop confidence from the experience of completing tasks.

Success should be measured not by parental goals or aspirations but by a child's beaming smile.

Children need to play with other children, on child-sized equipment in a child-sized environment of color and softness and safety. One early injury, fear, or failure can affect the child for a long time.

For children I don't recommend private lessons, especially if Mom or Dad is the prospective teacher. A well-intentioned adult may give patient and skilled instruction, but what children perceive in a private tutor is a larger, infinitely more capable adult model whom they cannot hope to emulate successfully. This can be very discouraging for a child. (On the other hand, watch how children delight in seeing Mom or Dad fumble, and how they laugh with glee when you let them feel stronger or smarter than you.) A good learning environment for a child is within a small group of other children, some more skilled and some less so.

Early play can help prepare a child for easier development later on, but the focus should remain on early *play* that feels good and not on intense training. It is also best to avoid early competitive emphasis.

Children can begin different kinds of movement training at different ages. The main factors determining when to start are the development of the bones and joints, the attention span, and natural interest. If your children are interested in some activity, let them try it, whether you have any interest in it or not, if they are willing to make a commitment for at least three months. On the other hand, if you start your child in an activity that only *you* are interested in, be prepared for eventual disappointment.

If your children are motivated—and if thay have been prepared well, it will take only about four or five years of serious training to approximate their highest level of achievement. The later years of training bring only subtle refinements and will not stabilize their attainments. You don't need, therefore, to start "budding Olympians" in long workouts before they are out of diapers.

Overinvolved parents who, in their loving enthusiasm, want to help their youngsters "a little too much" can often do as much harm as good. Too much interest on the part of parents can confuse children and weaken their motivation because they are never sure whether participation comes from their own interest or they are just living out a parental fantasy. Children under parental pressure will feel this internal contradiction no matter what their parents assure them; they can be acutely sensitive to parental feelings (far more than they appear to be) and are quick to see through the social lie that we may believe.

What you can offer your children is emotional and financial support, transportation to classes, and confidence in their learning process. It's great to go to a game occasionally, but if you get too zealous or wildly excited when your children win, they are going to feel that you're equally disappointed in them when they lose.

Whether or not your children are naturally inclined to active sports, or music, or martial arts, or dance, they can benefit from a regular form of training—of the body, mind, and emotions. There is something for every child; it is for them and their parents to discover what fits the children's personalities.

> *Treat children as though*
> *they are already the people*
> *they are capable of becoming.*
> —*HAIM GINOTT*

Sound preparation and the magic of time helps both adults and children to realize their fullest potential.

TWO
Developing Talent

**Everyone has a talent;
but rare is the courage
to follow the talent
to the places it leads.**
—ERICA JONG

Every time I taught at a gymnastics camp, I observed gymnasts who practiced diligently but met frustrating obstacles because they had not developed those key qualities that could have raised their potential and ease of learning. The athletic stars on television are products of natural selection, the few who rose above the hundreds or thousands who dropped out.

If we just engage in an activity and keep practicing, over time the qualities necessary for success begin to emerge. This might in fact seem to be the most "natural" approach, except for one catch: We all like to feel successful; we thus enjoy working on and demonstrating our strong points—and we tend to avoid practicing our weak points in the heat of the game. Our usual pattern is to let a strength in one sphere compensate for a weakness in another. This tactic may appear to work at beginning and intermediate levels, but eventually, undeveloped skills interfere with advanced skills. By emphasizing talent drills early in our careers and before every game, we can build a well-rounded foundation.

Athletes save a lot of time in the long run by developing talent first. Tom Weeden, as a freshman in high school, decided that he wanted to become a top gymnast, so he sought advice from every coach he could find. I was one of those coaches and suggested that he begin by developing strength, suppleness, and correct fundamentals before he concentrated on skill development—advice I had shared with many young athletes. Tom had the patience and wisdom to actually follow this advice. No one heard from Tom for about a year—then "all of a sudden" he "appeared on the scene," winning every competition around. Tom attended a top university on a gymnastics scholarship as one of the nation's finest gymnasts.

An overnight success
usually takes about ten years.
          —ANONYMOUS

No matter what you imagine your limitations to be—no matter what your body looks or feels like now, even if you've been in a slump for a year—if you're willing to undergo the initiation necessary to develop your talent, you will become a natural athlete. All the qualities are within you native to you. You may have to direct more energy and time than someone else in order to bring out the proper qualities, but you certainly have the capacity to do it.

Since we all intuitively understand the value of preparation, this advice may seem obvious. Yet few of us act on the basis of our understanding in our haste to achieve flashy skills, because preparation isn't as exciting, or because we don't understand how to build a foundation of mental, emotional, and physical talent.

The next three chapters provide a map of the talent process, beginning with the master key: the mind.

4 *Mental Talent*

The mind leads the body.

—KOICHI TOHEI

**Golf is twenty percent technique
and eighty percent mental.**

—BEN HOGAN

Perhaps you remember a time when you were lost in thought. Someone may have been talking with you, and you suddenly realized that you "hadn't heard a thing." At another time you might even have driven through a red light without seeing it. On occasions like these, your ears were functioning and your eyes were open, but your *attention was captured* by thought. Your attention can go in two fundamental directions: *outward*, to the world of energy and movement, or *inward*, to thoughts. For most of us, attention bounces randomly back and forth from inner concerns to outer realities.

Psychotics serve as an extreme example of people completely "lost in thought." For them, the habit of turning attention inward is so compelling that they have lost the capacity to maintain contact with external reality as we know it.

In contrast, most of us are able, with relative consistency, to direct our attention out into the world, but to a lesser degree, we're subject to the same liability as psychotics. We're distracted by mental noise as our attention drifts out of the present to the past or future.

If you sit down in a quiet room and close your eyes, you'll soon begin to notice many subtle stimuli that are normally below your conscious recognition. You may notice little aches or areas of tension. You'll become aware of your breathing and the expansion/release of your diaphragm and chest muscles. You'll notice the rhythmic beating of your heart and, eventually, more subtle internal displays of sound and light. But above all else, you'll notice the stream of thought that flows on and on and on.

Most of us are subject to a pattern of random attention, floating back and forth between the world and our inner content—the stream of reverie, fantasy, concerns, plans, fears, anger, expectations, sorrow, regrets, and rehearsals. The adult mind is full of compulsive, random (and usually problematic) thinking. Emotionally charged or disturbing thoughts take the shape of worry, fear, and anger; such thoughts impose tension on the body. You can test the truth of this in your own experience.

Thinking. . . is what gets you caught from behind.
        —*O.J. SIMPSON*

How can you think and hit at the same time?
        —*YOGI BERRA*

If something happens that we don't like—something that conflicts with our beliefs, expectations, or values—we become angry. We don't necessarily want to become angry, but we get angry just the same, as a reaction—not to what has occurred but to our own thoughts about whatever stimulated the upset. Others might not become disturbed by the same occurrence because they have different thoughts about it or values relating to it.

We've all experienced reactions of jealousy, sorrow, worry, and fear; we don't want to become obsessed with such thoughts and reactions, but we do nevertheless.

It may seem as if various wrongs in the world are the source of our disturbances, but if we examine our habit patterns closely, we see that our mind's resistance to circumstance is the seed of our discontent. Pushing distracting thoughts away is not always easy.

> **Meditation student:** I'm feeling upset.
> **Teacher:** You're reacting to a passing thought. Forget it.
> **Student:** I can't seem to forget it.
> **Teacher:** Then let it go.
> **Student:** I can't let it go either.
> **Teacher:** Then just just drop it.
> **Student:** I can't drop it!
> **Teacher:** Well, then I guess you'll just have to throw it out.

Inner athletes have learned, within their chosen arena, to focus their attention on the matter at hand—the next pitch, the next down, the next swing or other movement—in the present moment. Although thoughts come and go, the inner athlete's attention remains free of inward distractions, focused on the here and now. We can also apply this skill, developed through the intensity of specific training, to the practice of daily life. *This "practice of the present moment" may be one of the greatest benefits of any form of training.*

Mental talent emerges as we gain facility in dissolving archaic habit patterns, so that we no longer feel compelled to pay attention to the obstructions and limitations that are primitive creations of our own mind. All rigid mental patterns manifest as tension and physical symptoms. Many athletes work to overcome physical symptoms—stretching, practicing relaxation techniques, and so on—helpful, if only remedial, activities. There is no profound value, for example, in stretching for twenty minutes a day and letting an uncontrolled mind tie the body in knots of tension the rest of the time. Stretching and relaxation are central elements of physical talent, but before utilizing them we have to deal with the source of physical symptoms.

—————————— **REALITY CHECK** ——————————

Take this amusing test: A door swings open before you, and you see a sink full of water. The stopper is in, and the water is running. The water begins to pour over the sink's edge. Do you turn off the water and pull the plug, or do you grab the mop?

Many athletes, and most people dealing with problems in daily life, spend a lot of time "mopping up"—that is, dealing with symptoms. An example is couples who argue constantly about various topics when they need to focus instead on communicating more effectively. That might clear the problems at their source.

Developing mental talent involves "pulling the plug" on the primary source of emotional turbulence and physical tension.

One effective way to appreciate our present state of mind is to contrast it with the mind of a typical three-month-old. Babies store many of the impressions of movement and energy they perceive in the world. But because they have no words, because they have no complex associations, beliefs, opinions, values, and attitudes *relative* to those impressions, they don't think much *about* anything. They neither philosophize, conceptualize, nor theorize. Their attention is entirely focused in the present moment, without judgment or expectation.

Young children are thus relatively free of the complex fears, angers, attachments, expectations, plans, biases, self-imagery, and self-criticism that characterize most adult minds. Perhaps that's why the Bible tells us that unless we "become like little children, we cannot enter the kingdom of heaven."

Babies are inner athletes in their clarity, relaxation, sensitivity, and openness to the environment—in their simple, direct approach to life, free of mental reaction or resistance. These qualities account not only for their relatively astounding learning abilities but also for their innate charm, appeal, and spontaneity. These same traits account for the effectiveness of the inner athlete.

When we quiet the mind,
the symphony begins.
        —ANONYMOUS

We all began life as movement masters, our minds free of meaning, naturally blissful in our pristine "ignorance"—until associations and preconceptions begin to inhibit the body and the learning process. Babies, for example, when learning how to stand, just stand up and fall down, stand up and fall down. They don't judge their performance or compare themselves to anyone else ("Oh, darn! I'm such a klutz! I'll bet the baby across the street is doing this a lot better!").

A first step in reclaiming our innate potential is by examining four obstructions that seem to plague most of us at one time or another. *They are limited self-concept, fear of failure, destructive self-criticism, and lack of one-pointed attention.* The following sections deal with these key mental obstructions.

Limited Self-concept

Those who believe they can
and those who believe they can't
are both right.

—ANONYMOUS

The self-fulfilling prophesy is named for a common psycholog-ical phenomenon—how our progress in life tends to be consis-tent with our expectations. If you expect or believe that you are a super dancer, that you aren't very likable, that you are a whiz kid at math—you will set in motion psychological processes that tend to make your expectations come true. Your level of achievement reflects your self-concept.

This self-fulfilling prophesy applies to any field of endeavor. If you expect to do poorly, you will be less moti-vated, less interested; you'll put in less time and energy and will thus perform poorly.

> *An example is the story of the self-limiting shoe sales-*
> *man who was given a one-hundred-square mile area in*
> *which to sell shoes. The first month he generated*
> *$10,000 worth of business. His supervisor was so*
> *pleased that he doubled the salesman's area the next*
> *month. Nevertheless, the salesman still sold only*
> *$10,000 worth of shoes. Upset, the supervisor cut his*
> *area to half its original size. That month the salesman*
> *still sold $10,000 worth of shoes.*
> *He had a $10,000-a-month self-concept.*

Every time a new group of children or adults begins one of my gymnastics classes, I see them acting out roles based upon their self-concept. A few people play the role of class leaders, get in front of the line, and show what they can do. Others may stand quietly at the end of the line, making remarks like "Oh, I'm not too coordinated."

Your self-concept differs as it relates to your activities in daily life. You probably have a fairly high self-concept in athletics (or you wouldn't have participated); you may have a lower one in auto mechanics, bookkeeping, painting, or writing.

What I want to demonstrate is that *self-concept* is no more real than the shadow of a shadow. Self-concept is an illusion that has been imposed upon you long ago, and it will overshadow your every endeavor until you can see it for what it is and cut through it.

In order to achieve all that is demanded of us
we must regard ourselves as greater than we are.
—*JOHANN VON GOETHE*

————————————— **A WISH LIST** —————————————

One way of battling destructive self-concepts is to write down a list of fifty qualities or abilities you possess, or activities in which you might like to engage more if you felt you would be successful in those activities. Once the list is complete, rate yourself on a scale of from 1 to 10, 1 being totally inept and 10 being world class. Don't limit yourself to writing down only those activities you actually perform; include activities you tend to avoid.

Once you've rated yourself, take a look at this reflection of your self-concept. Examine the low self-ratings. Do you enjoy any of the activities in which you rated yourself low? Why or why not? Have you ever *really* put effort into these activities in order to become proficient? Is there any good reason you *really* couldn't become very good at any of these skills? People with no arms have become excellent painters; I've seen a one-legged man become a fine springboard diver; blind people have

excelled at running marathons and bouncing on the
trampoline. What's your excuse?

Here's final step in this exercise: When you finish
this chapter, sit quietly and consider the main points
about illusory self-concept. Look over your list and
self-ratings one more time. Then *burn that list.*

Through insight into the limiting nature of our self-concepts, we can overcome self-imposed limitations, which are
often based upon parental conditioning or upon a misinter-
preted incident.

Then, and only then, can our techniques or training have
any real momentum.

As a child, you were *pure potential* and could learn anything within human capacity. You had within you the seeds
of being a physician, an attorney, an engineer, a craftsman, a
dancer, an artist, or an Olympian. It never occurred to you
that learning was difficult. You were free from assumed limitation, like a story told to me by Jim Fadiman:

> *My four-year-old daughter decided that she wanted to learn
> to fly. It seemed elementary enough to her—even birds
> could do it. She stood on the couch and jumped, her arms
> flapping. Her first attempt was not entirely successful.*
>
> *She reasoned that since birds have feathers, this must
> be the missing ingredient. She found a feather in the yard.
> Holding it in her little hand, she leaped again into the air.
> She told me that the feather had "definitely helped."*

In letting his daughter attempt to fly from the couch, Jim
was allowing her to explore safely her *natural* powers and limitations. In this way she was able to gain a balanced, realistic
view of her abilities, uncolored by other people's expectations.
When I asked her father why he hadn't just saved her some

effort and explained to her that "little girls and boys can't fly," he replied, smiling, "How could I know? I might have been wrong."

When we were very young, we were free to learn, open to anything. As we grew, however, we began to get impressions that we were "good" at some things and "bad" at others—because we were praised and blamed, or because we misunderstood the situation—as I did when I was five.

In kindergarden painting class, I made my first picture of a tree. It looked like a green lollipop, since it was my first try. Then I looked around at the paintings of the other children, and to my disappointment, *their* paintings looked like *trees*. I didn't understand that they had drawn many more trees than I had. I didn't realize that, if I continued to practice as much as they had, my trees might look even more leafy than theirs. But I gave up too soon. Then and there, I decided that I was not a good painter.

Little Sammy formed a self-concept in another way. He was reaching for a glass of milk. Being three years old, he misjudged the distance and knocked the milk over. His mother, momentarily upset, said, "Oh, clumsy child!" This word "clumsy" was new to Sammy. He figured it had something to do with milk.

On another occasion, it happened again—but this time, with juice. "Clumsy!"

"Ah," Sammy reasoned. "It doesn't mean milk, it means *spilling* that makes me clumsy." Soon he had several dozen glasses of spilled liquid and a few falls down flights of stairs to *prove* it.

> *Sometimes . . . you feel that you can do anything. At times like this I can run up to the front of the board, stand on the nose pushing out through a broken wave; I can . . . put myself in an impossible position then pull out of it, simply because I feel happy. Confidence like that can carry you through things that are just about impossible.*
>
> —MIDGET FARRELLY

The undesirability of a low self-concept may seem obvious, since it limits our achievement. Unrealistically high self-concept has its own unique problems. Young children who are constantly praised for everything and told they are "the best" and "great" get used to such praise, which represents the positive attention that all children crave. They will strive to maintain this praise as much as possible; maybe they'll even develop precocious abilities.

The shadow side of this picture is that their sense of self-worth depends at first on the praise and later gets transferred to the achievement that earned the praise. They grow up to expect success, and they project this expectation onto other people, so that everyone in the world expects them to succeed. This expectation becomes a tremendous pressure not to let the world down. It can create brilliant students, star athletes, and suicides.

Unrealistically high *or* low self-concept create problems. The best self-concept is none at all. Children raised in a home relatively free from exaggerated praise or blame form a realistic, experimental, and persevering approach to their pursuits, without undue psychic pressure. They explore life, and they achieve out of a natural and innate sense of curiosity and internal satisfaction rather than external stroking or reward. They achieve naturally, enjoyably, without undue stress, in their own good time.

As you have perhaps noticed, we adults have an ample supply of self-concepts relative to our activities. Whenever you feel underconfident or confused about a specific endeavor, if you feel discouraged, or if you feel strong *pressure to do well,* an arbitrary self-concept is imposing itself on your life, obscuring the sense of ease and enjoyment you possessed as a child.

The next time this occurs, you can surrender to it, you can ignore it, you can resist it, or you can use it. If you surrender to it, your past will become your future. If you ignore it, the negative self-concept will continue to have subtle effects. If you resist it, you'll waste energy. *Use* it fully. Experience its psychic force, then cut through it by *changing your act. Learn to do what you didn't believe you could,* and the word "can't" will lose its power over your life.

Developing a realistic self-concept is the primary value of challenge courses like the firewalk, or skydiving, or the high ropes courses taught around the country. I teach a residential intensive training that uses knife-fighting skills to develop deeper levels of self-trust, courage, commitment, and flexibility. In courses like those mentioned, participants have a chance to confront limiting beliefs, then to transcend them.

When we say, "I'm not interested in doing that," what we often *feel* behind that statement is "I can't do well at that." When "can't" loses its force, you would be amazed at how many things you suddenly become interested in.

Using affirmations is one way to open your life to new possibilities. With an affirmation you make a positive statement to yourself, for example: "I am an accurate putter." "I perform even better under pressure." "I remember names and faces of the people I meet." "I enjoy not smoking, and I don't need to smoke."

These statements may seem like bold-faced lies, because every time we state them, *other secondary beliefs arise that seem to contradict these positive statements. By noticing these underlying contradictory beliefs, even exaggerating them, we bring them out into our consciousness where they can dissolve.* In making a positive statement that may not yet be true factually, we are opening the door to new possibilities and creating a pressure to change in the direction of our affirmation.

In order to amplify the effectiveness of any positive statement, picture in detail its most positive manifestation. Our subconscious doesn't know the difference between what we visualize and what is "real"—what we see with our physical eyes—so the more we visualize the positive outcomes, the more we draw that energy to ourselves and open our subconscious to attracting wonderful outcomes into our life. When I was competing in gymnastics I spent a lot of time visualizing myself going through fantastic routines; I believe this habit accounted for much of my success.

Success breeds success because it undermines assumed limitation.

And remember that the natural law of process is stronger than any self-concept. If you practice over time, you *will* improve. Transcending self-concept is a primary step on the path of the inner athlete.

Fear of Failure

Failure is an integral part of the learning process—a natural signpost, a guide, an aid to further progress. I used to "fail" at least fifty times a day in the gym; it was no big deal. In order to learn, we have to see what's not working and take it into account. Most of us, when still young, were taught to fear failure—especially public failure—and to avoid it at all costs. We have therefore built in some mechanisms of defense against failure.

A common defense against failure is "not really trying." Athletes who sometimes appear lazy may not be motivated. Why not? Usually because they don't feel they can succeed; they fear they will fail. If they do, they can fall back on the belief, "I could have succeeded if I'd really tried."

Fear produces tension; tension constricts the blood flow and slows the reflexes, producing shallow breathing resulting in general or chronic contraction of opposing muscle groups; it can even affect eyesight. All this change obstructs effective movement and leads to probable failure. Fear of failure thus produces a vicious circle, resulting in the occurrence of what was most feared.

To break this cycle, we need to make peace with failure, for failure is not our enemy. Yet it isn't enough merely to tolerate failure. "Tolerate" means to endure something; we need to *appreciate* failure in order to make use of it. When we learn something, let's give ourselves a couple dozen errors "for free." Let's even miss on purpose, just to stay loose and keep a balanced perspective. If we can make ourselves miss, we can also make ourselves hit.

Inner athletes laugh at failure as if it were an old friend playing a practical joke. The greatest inventors, artists, and athletes of all time failed many times. A lot of people know that Babe Ruth was the home-run king; they seldom realize that he was also the strike-out king.

You can impress this principle upon yourself with the following exercise, which is a cinch physically but a challenge psychologically: Fail on purpose. If you're a salesman, blow your next sales attempt. Just have fun and let go of any concern. Next time you go eighteen holes, see if you can double your golf score. Make mistakes you'd normally fear making. Have fun with failure and see if the sky falls in. (It won't.) Soon you'll improve "by accident."

Destructive Self-Criticism

Others will underestimate us,
for although we judge ourselves
by what we feel capable of doing,
others judge us only by
what we have already done.
     —LONGFELLOW

If babies carried around the same tendency toward self-criticism as adults, they might never learn to walk or talk. Can you imagine infants stomping the floor and saying, "Darn! Screwed up again!" Fortunately, babies are free of self-criticism. They treat failure the same as success; they just keeping practicing.

Self-criticism is a learned habit pattern, one that usually begins in childhood, since children naturally make errors and are often the target of destructive criticism.

There are only three causes of error in the world:

1. negative (or unconscious) habit patterns;
2. lack of information or experience;
3. the fact that no one is perfect all the time.

There are two kinds of criticism:

1. constructive: "You were a little too high on that one; try swinging lower on the next."
2. destructive: "That's all wrong—boy, that was dumb!"

If you received destructive criticism as a child, it is very likely that your young psyche used the most available defense; you *internalized* that criticism—that is, you began to criticize *yourself* severely so that others would refrain from doing so. This defense of childhood usually "works": it does tend to deflect criticism from parents, brothers, sisters, or playmates. But this archaic habit of criticizing yourself to prevent others from doing it is no longer useful; if you criticize yourself, you're still carrying around the weight of that parent, brother, sister, or playmate who was unkind to you.

You may not be fully aware that you are a victim of your own self-criticism, since you won't always yell or kick yourself; you may "beat yourself up" in more subtle ways, such as generating impatience, frustration, or depression.

We use self-criticism on ourselves in the same way others once used criticism on us: as punishment for errors. People who criticize themselves share a belief that if they punish themselves in this way, they will improve. Just the opposite is true. If you criticize (punish yourself) after making an error, the psychological scoreboard is even: "One error, one punishment." You are free to make the same error again. By not criticizing yourself, you are taking responsibility and are *less* likely to repeat the error.

Instead of fighting yourself, see if you can be your own best friend.

Be gentle with yourself. If you will not be your own unconditional friend, who will be? If you are playing an opponent and you are also opposing yourself, you are going to be outnumbered.

Maintain an attitude of *unconditional self-worth*, free from self-criticism. You can agree that it is cruel and unnecessary to tell someone else, "You are really stupid—what a klutz—you should give up—you keep making the same mistakes—you'll never be any good!" If you would never say those things to anyone else, *why not pay yourself the same courtesy?*

One-Pointed Attention

There is tremendous power in *total attention* to the matter at hand. But such quality of attention is relatively rare—except in the intensity of performance or competition when we focus our mind on the present moment, forgetting all else. Athletes may have problems in daily life—issues in relationships, or in the financial arena, for example—but when they find themselves in action, they experience the power of the present moment. In the moment of truth, we can each find moments of silence. Even while engaged in intense activity, we can feel internal serenity.

Athletes who achieve one-pointed attention feel totally "on," completely present. That state has been called "flow"; it has also been called "the zone." But whatever we call it, the inner athlete calls it "home."

> *When I play my best golf, I feel as if I'm . . . standing back watching the earth in orbit with a golf club in my hands.*
> **—MICKEY WRIGHT**

When skiers and surfers feel this total attention, they know they won't fail. Golfers in this state can almost "see" lines of energy from the ball to the hole. Tennis players in "the zone" anticipate what is going to happen before it happens.

In daily life, for most of us, attention is diffused and distracted by thought; our minds are half on what we're doing and half on thoughts about what we're doing, or in random daydreams. In fact, our lives can feel a lot like a dream.

As we learn to notice, and finally access, one-pointed attention to the present moment through our the ability to use it, it lifts the quality of our sport. Inner athletes who expand this ability to "come home to the here and now" lift the quality of daily life.

> *You completely ignore everything and just concentrate. You forget about the whole world and just . . . are part of the car and the track. It's a very special feeling. You're completely out of this world. There's nothing like it.*
>
> —*JOCHEN RINDT*

———————— MIND AND BODY ————————

The following exercise shows how even a subtle distraction affects the body: Ask a friend to stand comfortably with his arms at his sides. Ask him to tense one arm, locking it straight and clenching his fist, with his arm pointed downward along the side of his body. Tell him you are going to try to pull his arm away from his body, sideways, for a foot or two. Do that, and notice the amount of effort required for you to pull the arm out.

Next, tell him that you are going to try to pull his arm away from his body, sideways, for a foot or two. Do that, and notice the amount of effort required for you to pull the arm out.

Next, tell him that you are going to wave your hand in front of him, with a zigzag motion downward, without touching him, and then you'll try immediately again to pull his arm outward as you did the first time. Proceed to do this.

Do you notice the difference? What happened to his mental focus when you made the distracting hand motion?

If your friend's attention can be distracted in this way, imagine what mental distractions can do to anyone's performance. Athletic training is the best school for one-pointed concentration because it demands our full attention in the present. Like the unstoppable focus of world-class athletes, inner athletes achieve the ability to follow through in sport or life, no matter what distractions assail them.

> *Obstacles are those frightful things we see when we take our eyes off the goal.*
> —*HANAH MORE*

If gymnasts fall off the beam, their minds have already fallen off. In order for them to maintain perfect balance, they must keep their minds (or attention) squarely over the beam. Before a football player can be stopped, his attention must be tackled. Any good tackle knows that some runners are more difficult to stop than others and that the phenomenon is not just a matter of physical conditioning, it is a matter of mental training.

> *I wasn't worried about a perfect game going into the ninth. It was like a dream. I never thought about it the whole time. If I'd thought about it I wouldn't have thrown a perfect game.*
> —*CATFISH HUNTER*

The following two-part exercise can show you the difference between weak attention-intent and total one-pointedness:

Test 1. Stand and squarely face a friend from a distance of about 10 feet. Let's say it's a male friend. His feet are shoulder-width apart, each the same distance from you. Now, assuming a timid stance, walk in a straight line, as if to brush past his right side. As you are about to pass him, he lifts up his right arm directly in front of your chest. Let your mind stop at the arm that is held in front of you.

Test 2. This time, do everything exactly the same, with one mental difference. Walking the same speed, project your attention with force a thousand miles in front of you. You therefore pay no attention to your friend's arm as it is raised; your mind and your forward motion continue right through the arm as if it weren't there: you are relaxed, positive, centered. What do you experience this time?

In this exercise you just completed, your friend's arm represents those little distractions of daily life, the thoughts that spring up to distract you. When you pay as little attention to thoughts of fear, anger, limitation as you did to your friend's arm, you'll be on your way to one-pointed attention.

Every basketball player has experienced the difference between shooting a basket with full attention and attempting the same with only partial concentration. If, for example, Stretch is about to shoot, and his attention is divided between the basket and the opponent guard behind him, he's likely to miss a shot he could do easily in practice. Experiment on your own with Trash-basketball:

TRASH-BASKETBALL

Sit about 10 feet away from a wastebasket. Crumple some waste paper into about twenty little balls. Get ready to play.

Step 1. Without paying real attention, casually toss some balls toward the basket, and see if any sink in.

Step 2. This time, focus your attention intently by staring in the center of the wastebasket. Sink your mind into the basket. Staying relaxed, toss a few balls in. (Remember not to "try" or you'll tense; just let them go in.) Check your results. Were you focused?

Step 3. Do the same as step 2, but once in a while, at random, have a friend standing behind you poke you in the ribs as you're about to shoot. Notice what that does to mental focus and your accuracy.

One-pointed attention brings freedom from internal distractions and problems and can help you master any game. Such mental power has tremendous carryover into the Game of Life. As you stabilize your ability to focus attention fully on the matter at hand, you find yourself resting more and more in the present moment. Free of internal complications, you'll find that daily life simplifies itself and feels more profound and full.

You completely ignore everything and just concentrate. You forget about the whole world and just . . . are part of the car and the track. It's a very special feeling. You're completely out of this world. There's nothing like it.

—*JOCHEN RINDT*

Freedom from mental distraction equals power. Olympic champion weightlifters don't just have powerful bodies; they have powerful minds. The same quality of attention frees us, in the moment of truth, from any thought of self-concept, criticism, or fear. Inner athletes eventually come to the realization that this and every moment, on or off the field, is the moment of truth.

> *You're involved in the action and vaguely aware of it, but your focus is not on the commotion but on the opportunity ahead. I'd liken it to a sense of reverie ... the insulated state a great musician achieves in a great performance ... not just mechanical, not only spiritual; something of both, on a different plane and a more remote one.*
>
> —ARNOLD PALMER

Training of the inner athlete doesn't take place automatically. We have to *isolate* mental qualities before we can develop them. If training is not fully conscious or systematic, it is random and haphazard. If you, for example, felt *something* wrong with your running as you loped around a track, but weren't able to pinpoint the specific problem, you would probably just continue training the body, as you had done before—striving to improve by doing more of the same.

But, as you learned in Chapter 2, The Power of Awareness, only when you identify a problem can you take appropriate steps to solve it.

Many golfers go through periods when they just can't seem to sink a putt. Tennis players have double-fault slumps. These frustrated athletes may look to the heavens, wondering why the gods are punishing them; they may start carrying rabbit's feet wrapped in garlands of four-leaf clovers; they may develop nervous tics or voluntarily commit themselves to rest homes—just because they can't identify the source of their problem.

Now that you have a better understanding of the mental

structures and mechanisms that influence your game, you don't ever need to become stuck in that kind of a slump.

And remember—sometimes when you seem to be vegetating, going nowhere, even slipping backward, you may just be backing up to get a running start.

With mind clear, the body is at its peak efficiency and awareness. When you are in action, it's best to "lose your mind and come to your senses."

In appreciating the mind's influence on movement, you're developing a map of understanding. Next, we look to the emotions, which furnish the *fuel* for your journey.

5 *Emotional Talent*

We may understand the journey; we may even have a sound vehicle; but on any journey—whether through athletics or in daily life—we need sufficient emotional fuel to get moving.

Different from physical-vital energy, emotional energy creates the *feeling impulse* to move toward our goals; we call it motivation. When emotional energy flows through us freely, without obstructions, we feel naturally motivated. There is no force more powerful than a motivated human being. We've all heard success stories about underdogs who produced miracles from the stuff of motivation. Motivation serves as a key to any process of training and beats at the heart of emotional talent.

> ***Nothing great was ever achieved***
> ***without enthusiasm.***
> ***—RALPH WALDO EMERSON***

Inspiration and motivation can make the difference between victory and defeat, success and failure, or even life and death. The energy derived from motivation carries distance runners past the "wall of pain" when their physical energy reserves are exhausted. On the other hand, strapping athletes bursting with vital physical energy who lack a directed emotional impulse to strive for their goals may wander aimlessly and arrive nowhere in particular.

We all appreciate the importance of self-discipline but think of discipline as doing what we don't really feel like doing. With sufficient motivation, we're so inspired that we don't even think about discipline. As a young gymnast, for example, I was so inspired and excited that I trained six days a week for more than four hours a day for years and never felt as if I were "working" or that I needed discipline. They key for me was to keep my eye on the shining goal that inspired me.

Once released, the power of emotional energy can work magic: It smothers fear and steamrolls over obstacles. An obstacle is just something we worry about when we've taken our eyes off the goal.

I've seen athletes who were long-shots develop into national champions through directed emotional energy. Eric, a teammate of mine, had had polio as a child. His legs were so atrophied that when I first saw him he had to walk with braces or on crutches. He became a specialist on the rings. He simply worked harder than anyone. It wasn't enough to develop superior strength; he also began to practice a dismount from the rings that took him about nine feet in the air. He performed a full-twisting somersault and, by some incredible feat of will, landed unassisted on those spindly legs. Over and over I'd see him crash to the floor. His brother told me he used to go home and cry, the pain in his legs was so intense. After three years, Eric was able to run around the gym without leg braces, and he placed second in the national championships.

In daily life, little tasks that require only a modest amount of energy do not require great motivation for their completion. The world of athletics, however, demands much more of us.

Most of us relate to motivation passively, as if it were something that descends upon us without our control. We might feel motivated on one day but not on another day. The

message of this chapter is that all the motivational energy we'll
ever need is within us.

Emotional talent is the capacity to stimulate and draw upon
one's natural fountain of energy. Developing emotional talent
is learning to blow into our own sails.

When we speak of emotions, we often refer to "positive"
emotions like joy, serenity, and elation, and "negative" emotions like fear, sorrow, or anger. The latter are not true emotions
at all but emotional obstructions that block the free and natural
flow of motivation. To understand this better, let's look back to
our infancy:

When we were babies, motivation was natural to us, and
it was constant, for everything was interesting to us. On occasion we might have tensed our little bodies and cried, but cry-
ing was a simple, natural response to physical discomfort, not
complex mental concerns. Our general state was a clear mind
and relaxed body. Our minds and bodies were in their natural
relationship—mind free of thought, in a state of clarity, focus, and
attention; body free of tension, full of feeling, sensitivity, and vitality. We experienced the state of pure energy—motivation—fuel
for action, the impulse to move, to explore, to grow.

As we grew and became more aware of the rules, meanings, and demands of the world, we began to feel a separation
from the protected cradle of infancy. Vulnerable to a world of
emotional turbulence, social turmoil, and human frustration,
we began to know guilt, fear, and anxiety. We learned to dam
up our emotions so that we didn't feel bad; in fact, we didn't
feel much at all. As minds become depositories of traumatic
memories, bodies begin to store tension. We experience this
tension as a cramp in the chest or abdominal region, but also in
the lower back, neck, jaws, and some other body parts. The
name of this tension, which we can observe in ourselves in
times of stress, is emotion. But the feeling we call "emotional"
is most often a blockage of emotional energy. Because that
energy is blocked, much as water flowing through a hose

might be blocked, we feel pressure at the points of tension.

The energy gathers in knots, taking shape as what we call anger or fear or sorrow, depending upon what thoughts stimulated that tension. Emotional blocks (or tension) are reactions to thoughts. If you're standing in line at the bank and someone butts in front of you, you may immediately "feel angry." Infants don't become upset by someone butting in line because they haven't yet incorporated society's responses to such an action. But you have learned that "people should wait their proper turn in line." Perhaps true enough, socially. Yet it is such meanings that stimulate emotional reactions. Only the mind free of meanings and judgments and expectations can allow the free flow of emotional energies—free of reactions of fear, sorrow, and anger.

Fear, sorrow, and anger are the three primary emotional obstructions, and like the three primary colors they combine to form a wide spectrum of such emotional hues as impatience, frustration, melancholy, and anxiety.

Fear, sorrow, and anger are normal, but they are not inevitable emotional reactions to perceived stress. Infants may cry from physical discomfort, but they are naturally free from the complex mental structures that often result in emotional tension.

Inner athletes do not deny or repress their feelings, but they learn to stay relaxed even under stressful conditions.

As it happens, it is very difficult to "feel" angry, fearful, and sorrowful if we breathe evenly and fully and we keep the body relaxed. Emotional upsets are inevitably associated with a tension in the chest or abdomen; by keeping relaxed and focusing on our breathing, we short-circuit the tension-producing stress. That allows us to express ourselves, or act, far more effectively.

If, for example, a growling dog jumps out at us with its teeth bared, it may be appropriate for us to freeze, run, growl back, or climb the nearest telephone pole. We can perform any of these natural reactions immediately, without the reactive tension we interpret as fear. And, in fact, such tension will only serve to delay the appropriate response.

It's healthy to express sorrow or anger or fear. But tension—emotional or otherwise—is not useful to the body. Its debilitating effects on blood circulation, muscle response, and the immune system have been well documented.

Breaking the Circuit of Tension

We have seen that the mind imposes tension on the body and is the source of emotional turmoil. But until we master the mind, how do we break the harmful circuit of mental stress that becomes emotional and physical tension?

Follow this technique to regain emotional equanimity:

—— **TENSE, SHAKE, BREATHE, AND RELAX** ——

- Deliberately tense your whole body as tightly as you can for three to five seconds, while holding your breath.

- Then gently shake your body.

- Next, stand tall, as if your head were suspended in space from a string, and breathe slowly, deeply, and evenly from your lower belly. Let the breath bring a sense of deep relaxation.

Undoing emotional habits formed over the years isn't easy, but we can do it. In any moment, you have the capacity to breathe deeply, relax, and let go. Allow rather than resist what arises inside or out in the present moment. Let it be interesting rather than "good" or "bad." In this way, we reawaken true emotion, the energy to *act*.

Breath and Feeling

"Inspiration," in addition to its usual connotation, also means to breathe in. The breath is a key to your emotional state because it both reflects and can control your level of tension. Learning to breathe properly, with full feeling, gives you the ability quite literally to "inspire" yourself. The natural athlete, like the infant, breathes naturally, from deep in the body, with slow, full, relaxed, and balanced inhalations and exhalations.

To understand your emotional state and to gain mastery over emotions, it's essential that you begin to observe and gain conscious control over your breathing. Breath awareness and discipline were central to the teachings of the most ancient spiritual traditions. Yogis, Zen masters, and martial artists have all placed great emphasis on breathing properly.

The one unifying link between mind and body is the breath. Meditation deals with the mind but could also be called a physical relaxation exercise. Relaxation exercises, in turn, deal with the body but could also be called meditation exercises. Both body and mind are intimately related to the emotions through awareness of the breath. The various approaches to well-being demonstrate the intimate relationship of the three centers: physical, mental, and emotional. Meditation practices center around insight and release of thought. As thoughts are released, emotions flow naturally, and the body relaxes. Coming from another direction, you can emphasize relaxation of the body. As the body relaxes, the mind tends to become quiet as well, and the emotions open. All the various approaches to well-being are only ways to reawaken the natural athlete within us.

If you were to observe your breathing for a few hours during the day, you would notice periods of fitful breathing, with starts and stops, holding of the breath, tension in the chest area, limiting the breathing to shallow gulps of air in the upper chest. If you studied your breathing—and that of others over a long period of time—you would see that the three primary emotion-

al obstructions—anger, sorrow, and fear—are each characterized by an imbalance in breathing. Anger is reflected by weak
inhalation and forceful, exaggerated exhalation. Sorrow (as in
sobbing) is characterized by spasmodic, fitful inhalation and
weak exhalation. Fear can result in very little breathing at all.
As you develop awareness of your breathing patterns through
conscious intent, you can become responsible for the recognition of reactive patterns as error and can then use the breath as
a key method of balancing body, mind, and emotions.

The following exercise will give you a feeling for proper
breathing and its effect on the body:

Sit comfortably, either on a chair or on a cushion. The
spine should be upright but not stiff.

Tension breathing. For a few minutes, breathe with
the shoulders raised upward; breathe using the upper
chest only; take shallow breaths. Experience how this
feels.

Natural breathing. Relax the shoulders by lifting
and dropping them a few times, until they just hang.
Feel their weight. Keep the mouth closed, the chin
tucked gently in, and the eyes closed.
    Breathe slowly and deeply, but without any sense
of strain. When you inhale, feel your belly draw
downward and slightly outward. When you exhale,
let the belly relax back up and in. Do this for at least
ten minutes, remembering to relax the shoulders, to
keep the mouth closed, to notice the rise and fall of
the belly. Experience what natural breathing feels
like.

As natural breathing becomes more natural for you, you can apply it to your athletic play and your everyday activities. Your breathing will soon be more conscious and timed rhythmically to the force and rhythm of your movements, giving them grace and ease. Ultimately, you will feel that your breath moves your body, freeing you from unnecessary muscular effort. Whenever you *notice* that you feel tense, just focus your attention on *feeling* the pleasure of slow, deep, relaxed breathing. Let the shoulders hang. In a few moments, you'll feel the change. Controlling the breath is but one of the ways we can exercise control over emotional reactivity—not by repressing but by transcending.

The Inner Witness

The law of accommodation reminds us that "life develops what it demands." The corollary of that principle says *what is not used becomes obsolete.* On the physical level, for example, if we don't use a muscle, it atrophies—it becomes weak. It's the same for reactive emotional habit patterns; through nonuse, we make them obsolete.

Witnessing is a learned skill consisting of recognition and release of old patterns. If we notice anger, we acknowledge it and release it.

It may seem strange, but we can feel good physically in spite of whatever negative thoughts or emotions arise. Negative thoughts don't have to mean negative tension—*if* we are willing to let go of them. That is the essence of witnessing.

Acknowledging an emotional obstruction—("I'm afraid," "I feel angry")—is constructive, even essential for optimal health. But meditating on that obstruction, habitually dramatizing it, creates an unwelcome pattern.

Fear, anger, and sorrow, are part of life. We don't make them go away by wishing it. But we do have the choice of ways we will respond.

We don't have to bring a fearful thought or its corresponding tension to *life*; we don't have to dramatize it. We may feel
afraid, but we don't have to act afraid. We don't have to freeze
or scream "OHMYGOD!" We need not act out the role of someone who is afraid.

It's not easy to refrain from dramatizing a reactive pattern.
But we can learn that it isn't necessary to wait passively for fearful thoughts to go away or "get better," nor is it necessary to
wait for emotions to disappear before we learn to act rather than
merely to react. All we need to do is change our actions. We
can speak positively and act positively, whether we feel like it or
not.

Inner athletes can't afford to hang on to compulsive or
reactive baggage. We don't want to ignore, resist, or repress that
baggage; it's certainly not helpful to pretend we don't feel its
weight. But we can translate our responses into positive energy
and action. Then start to experience motivation as our natural
state in everything we do.

> **When we feel willing and eager**
> **the gods join in.**
>   —*AESCHYLUS*

6 *Physical Talent*

**Ambition by itself never gets anywhere
until it forms a partnership with hard work.**

—JAMES GARFIELD

Just as mental clarity lights our path and emotional energy furnishes our fuel, the body provides the *vehicle* for action. Even if we understand the road and our tanks are full, we need a vehicle to take the journey. Golfers with clear minds and inspired emotions, for example, still have to learn to swing the club if they are going to play the game! To put it another way:

> *Success is sweet, but
> it usually has the scent of sweat about it.*
> *—ANONYMOUS*

Our Most Prized Possession

Take a moment to appreciate your body; take a lifetime. There is no greater miracle in nature. Its complexities fill encyclopedias, and still there's more to be said. Just as the universe contains millions of bodies, your body may contain millions of universes. We are made of the same stuff as stars. Each time we breathe, we are breathing in molecules breathed out by Jesus, Mohammed, the Buddha, Joan of Arc.

Your body has a brain that can contemplate the cosmos over breakfast, write a sonnet over tea. If there is a cosmic instruction manual, the first rule is surely that we each receive a body. It is the only thing you are guaranteed to keep for a lifetime—not your house, your car, your money, your relationships, your friends, or even your beliefs. You get to keep only your body. It is the only thing you "own," and, as it turns out, it's only on lease. The hand that holds this book is the only one you will ever have in this life.

Whatever our beliefs, we can know for sure that we have this life, this body. We need to remember that our body's warrantee is limited, good for a short time only. Let's look at the body's care, feeding, and development.

Leverage for Change

Because our minds and emotions are difficult to observe and tend to resist change, the body is an ideal, highly-visible medium for transformation. As it turns out, if we work with the body in positive ways, that work also helps the mind and emotions. When we relax the body and release tensions, the mind and emotions tend to reflect this change (and vice versa). *Conscious physical training is using the visible to mold the invisible.*

This chapter addresses the means to increasing our physical talent for athletics and life. In exploring physical talent, let's first consider what we mean by getting into shape. Our view of what constitutes "good shape" has changed over the years.

In the early 1900s, those of us who lived in the West defined fitness by means of outer strength and musculature. Big muscles, big chests, and big, brawny men were considered "fit." In recent years, more sophisticated research on stress, exercise, and diet have led us to reconsider this view. Dr. Kenneth Cooper certainly popularized the importance of cardiovascular fitness and aerobic activities. We know that the life expectancy for professional football players is considerably less than for the general public despite their size and musculature, perhaps in part because of the physical abuse inherent in a combative game but also because of other lifestyle factors, such as diet.

In response to current knowledge communicated to the public through the media, more of us are achieving higher levels of fitness (partly defined by longevity) through adopting low-fat diets, abstaining from tobacco and other drugs, abstaining from or moderating use of alcohol, and engaging in aerobic-type activities.

Our knowledge of "fitness" is incomplete, however. We are still rediscovering ancient wisdom about fitness in the Eastern traditions of India and Asia (particularly in certain martial arts traditions). We are going deeper into the body, from the outer layers of musculature into the heart and lungs and still deeper into the recesses of the nervous system.

Growing evidence in psychoneuroimmunology (psychosomatic or mind-body medicine), which acknowledges the influence of the brain-mind on the neuromuscular, hormonal, endocrine, and immune systems, leads us to redefine fitness not just as the ability to do work or even as longevity but as a state of serenity, plenitude, and expansiveness (inner peace). We are beginning to ask ourselves, "What good is it if we are slim and muscular (or even wealthy and famous) if we feel stressed, insecure, anxious, or addicted to achievement?"

Physical fitness exercises of the future will center around forms of conscious exercise that include, or are evolved from, forms of hatha yoga, breathwork, meditation, and ever-more-sophisticated forms of bodywork and refined physical disciplines (including Feldenkreis and Alexander work, Hellerwork and other forms of deep-tissue massage, aromatherapy, colortherapy, biofeedback, acupuncture and acupressure, and hundreds of other names, styles, and offshoots of systems exploring healing and bridging the mind-body connection).

We have seen aerobics classes evolve from high-impact activities to non-impact, flowing movement, often incorporating sophisticated warmups, cooldowns, deep relaxation, martial arts, and meditation. In the next generation, we will see the emphasis of sports and games change to less competitive and more cooperatively challenging.

Where "no pain, no gain" was once respected, aware teachers are now showing how to progress within one's comfort zone, without stress, without cycles of fatigue and strain to recovery.

Reshaping the Body

Our bodies are malleable; we can sculpt them over time according to our daily habits of diet and exercise. The body may change slowly, but it *will* change (as per the law of accommodation). Inner athletes' training includes aligning the body's shape and movements to natural forces. Look, for example, at your body's relationship to gravity. There are only two stable positions in gravity: horizontal and vertical. If your body is lying flat or standing straight, it's naturally aligned in gravity. If the body is out of line, however—if it has poor posture—then extra energy is required to keep it stable in the pull of gravity. To maintain your position you would need to lean on something or someone, or else exert muscular effort.

Take a moment to stand up, then lean forward or sideward or backward a few degrees, from the waist—or just stick your head forward a few inches—you'll soon feel a pressure or slight tension in the muscles that must now work to hold the spine vertical. If you held that position for a few minutes or more, it would soon become painful.

> *Exercise is only as beneficial*
> *as the posture in which we perform it.*
> —*JOSEPH HELLER*

--- **GETTING STRAIGHT** ---

For ten minutes, while sitting, standing, or moving, see if you can maintain a tall, stretched, erect posture, with a long back, chin gently tucked in, back of head stretched upward, with shoulders relaxed. Notice whether this is easy or difficult for you.

If you're like most of us, your body is probably out of line, deviating to some degree from perfect vertical alignment. This misalignment can be a result of childhood accidents, incorrect movement patterns and compensations, occupational or sports imbalances, or even emotional traumas that resulted in stored tensions and shortened muscles.

Aggressive persons often hold their heads or chins slightly forward as a result of chronic tension and shortened muscles in the back of the neck. If you injured an ankle years ago and began to favor it, you may have caused compensatory reactions up through the knee, hip, and shoulders. Some people have a pattern of holding the belly in or pulling the pelvis back, each causing misalignment in gravity.

These or similar postural imbalances within the field of gravity result in chronic tension. Energy is wasted, since muscular effort is constantly required to hold the body up. Fatigue sets in too often and too much. (Of course, diet, sleep habits, and other variables can also contribute to fatigue—but postural imbalance is a major source of energy drain.)

Constant physical tension may go unnoticed, since we become accustomed to it over the years, but it results in a chronic sense of discomfort, with constant shifting and fidgeting, nervousness, and even emotional irritability. The body feels less comfortable to "live in."

Stress and fatigue are expressed in other symptoms, ranging from tension headaches to lower back pain. The stored tensions produce a hardening of the connective tissue and lowered blood circulation, resulting in limited mobility or stiffness.

Many systems of massage, exercise, and manipulation can aid our conscious efforts to realign our bodies. If our connective tissue has become shortened as a result of chronic tension, it does little good to "try" to have good posture, because as soon as we relax, the shortened tissue will pull the body parts into the habitually misaligned position. In many cases, therefore, deep tissue work and chiropractic manipulation can be useful. While massage uses pressure and stroking to temporarily relax and release chronic tension, deep tissue massage works with lengthening the fascia or connective tissue around the muscles, for more lasting results.

Conscious Exercise

Unlike most outer-directed sports and games centered around points and scores, conscious exercise is inner-directed—specifically designed for overall balance and the well-being of the body, mind, and emotions.

If we're very strong but inflexible, hatha yoga, dance, or another form of stretching practice will serve to extend our range of motion. On the other hand, if we're naturally flexible, specific strength-building exercises will better serve our overall balance through muscular control and joint stability. Our bodies respond naturally to well-balanced and regular exercise.

– HANGING: BALANCING GRAVITY'S CRUNCH –

Without gravity, you'd soon become a mass of mush, without muscle tone, with weak circulation of blood and lymph, totally susceptible to any unusual stresses on the body. The field of gravity is the Great Developer, a twenty-four-hour exercise laboratory. Astronauts must exercise or create artificial gravity, or else their bones deossify.

On the other hand, gravity's pull can also be debilitating. You are being compressed all day; the vertebrae are pressed, one against the other, with only small pads between them, and your feet bear a great burden. Your joints are compressed hour after hour.

The simplest way to balance gravity's crunch is to *hang* every day. In the morning and evening, grab hold of a bar or solid door sill . . . or make a simple hanging bar that will easily support your weight. Hang for ten seconds to a half minute. Feel the joints opening, the spine gently stretching out.

Resistance to Change

Our bodies, like our minds and emotions, have a tendency to resist change. We settle into certain patterns of movement and behavior, and only conscious effort can change these patterns.

Resistance is related to Newton's law of inertia and momentum, which states, "A body at rest tends to stay at rest, and a body in motion tends to stay in motion, unless acted upon by external force." To translate that into the kind of resistance to change I'm talking about, we might say, "A body that begins in balance tends to stay in balance, and a body out of balance tends to stay that way, too . . . unless acted upon by an outside force."

Any change, therefore, requires an initial period of discomfort, until the body adjusts to the new demand. We experience this discomfort as we develop any new talent; we may feel symptoms ranging from fatigue to sore muscles. The pain may be mild in some cases, like the hunger pangs we feel when we streamline the diet; it can be more severe, as in withdrawal symptoms experienced when breaking a drug habit. In any case, symptoms are signs of the body readjusting; they will pass.

In changing to a new pattern of diet or exercise or life habits, the initiatory period may last from one to six weeks or even longer. By the end of that time, we'll have adapted to a new pattern. The period of stabilization, however, takes from three to six months. During this period, it's important to maintain our desire, motivation, and commitment by visualizing the goal— by letting it inspire us.

Unless the desire to change remains strong, body and mind will tend to return to old patterns. Dieters tend to return to old patterns; so do smokers, unless they maintain the new pattern for a period of stabilization. Be patient and persistent, because it takes time for old habits to become obsolete.

The laws of process, balance, and natural order all point to the obvious: We absolutely can reshape our life patterns and our bodies through insight, direction, and energy—when mind and emotions (motivation) work in harmony to generate strong will. When we see clearly what must be done and have a realistic sense of the challenge involved in change, then we are more likely to succeed. The greatest challenge often involves our own bodies.

Feeding the Physical Self

Our bodies are "fed" on many levels—through sunlight and fresh air, through peaceful environments, and through affection and energy from friends and family as well as through the food we eat. All these factors are equally important for us to thrive as a complete human being—but the most visible need is to be fed through the intake, digestion, and assimilation of food. The food we eat has a great influence on the shape, function, and overall talent of our bodies.

How you eat is as important as *what* you eat. The complete cycle of nourishment begins when food is taken in and continues with its digestion, distribution to where it's needed, utilization of the nutrients, and elimination of toxic wastes. Any weakness in this complete cycle can fundamentally affect your well-being. Emotional calm, proper eating habits, and appropriate time and place to eat are therefore as important to consider as the food itself.

I am amazed by friends who are extremely conscious of the quality of food they eat; yet they often eat when rushed or when anxious. Many activity-oriented people have the same problem; they find it difficult to really take a "time out" when they sit down to eat—or they don't sit down at all!

Every aspect of the food cycle is important. That doesn't mean we have to become nutritional scientists. Even little babies, whose instincts are intact, will choose the proper combination of foods for proper nutrition if offered a variety.

Pre-civilized humans ate whatever foods were in season, when they were fresh, without chemical additives, preservatives, or commercial processing. The processing, preserving, coloring, and sweetening that characterize many foods today are commercial practices designed to make higher profits by preventing spoilage and loss and also to attract buyers accustomed to bright colors and extra sweetness. Whether all this processing adds or detracts from the quality of the food is something you'll have to decide for yourself as you refine and come to trust your instincts.

Many experts know a lot about food, but you are the expert on your own body. Some "good foods" like whole wheat bread may not be good for you if you happen to be allergic to whole wheat (or wheat gluten), for example.

The reason so many of us need reshaping in the first place is because we tend to eat *too much of what we don't need and not enough of what we do need.* Many of us use food as a consolation when we're feeling upset or bored.

At some point in their own development, athletes need "high octane" fuel, and they start to simplify their diet; they start to notice the difference between what they want and what they need. As this process of sensitizing the body's instincts continues, many athletes find they feel better— lighter, with better endurance, by eating less meat.

In fact, the belief that athletes (or anyone) need "lots of protein" is a fantasy. Every protein-related illness in our country is related to excess protein, not to a lack of it. Nor do we need to carefully combine different foods, or eat lots of meat, or (for vegetarians) even eat a lot of tofu. Anyone who eats a balanced diet of fruits, vegetables, grains, and legumes is going to get plenty of protein.

Although I happen to eat a vegan (pronounced VAY-GAN) diet, without any kind of meat or dairy product, eating that way isn't my religion; it's just a simplified, healthful diet for me. I've maintained an excellent level of fitness, health, and youthful appearance for my age.

John Robbins, author of the classic book, *Diet for a New America* (Stillpoint), helped dispell the myth that athletes need meat.

He describes athletes like Dave Scott, of Davis, California, a scholar-athlete who won Hawaii's legendary Ironman Triathlon a record four times. Many consider Dave Scott the fittest man who ever lived. Scott is a vegetarian.

Sixto Linares, also a vegetarian, broke the world record

for a "double Ironman"—in one day, by swimming 4.8 miles, cycling 185 miles, then running 52.4 miles.

Robert Sweetgall of Newark, Delaware, another vegetarian, is the world's premier ultra-distance walker. So is Edwin Moses, *Sports Illustrated's* Sportsman of the Year.

We might not expect to find a vegetarian in world championship body-building competitions, but Andreas Cahling, 1980 Mr. International, is a vegetarian, and has been for over ten years of highest level international competitions.

Robbins cites a great many other examples of sports champions in many fields who do not eat meat.

My own experience is similar. While I was in college and recovering from a serious motorcycle accident, I stopped eating meat. I was the only one of my teammates who even considered such a "radical" course; my coach assured me it was just a fad; my doctor (who, like most physicians, had never taken a single nutrition course in medical school), told me I needed "liver and other meats" to help my leg recover. But my dietary change felt so good that I trusted my instincts. A year later, as one of the strongest gymnasts in the nation, I helped lead my team to the National Collegiate Championships.

Each of us has his or her own destiny to live—our own choices regarding our sport, art, relationships, hobbies, and diet. I respect each person's process. Even though yoga may have wonderful benefits, I would not suggest to a football player, for example, that he should be doing hatha yoga or T'ai Chi instead because he would be healthier. If he loves football, then that is what he should be doing. In the same spirit, I only share my experience and research; I do not presume to tell people what they should or shouldn't eat or do. We each need to make our own choices, based upon what we understand, feel, and need in our own lives. What I share in this or any book is to help readers make educated choices in their own lives.

But over time, if you simplify your diet in the direction of fresh, natural, unprocessed foods, trusting your instincts, your body will become more sensitive, and you won't need experts to tell you what you should eat. You'll begin to want to eat just what you need—instead of needing to eat just what you want.

No one can escape the operations of natural law. If you eat healthful food, full of its original nutritional value, and if you eat properly, that food will contribute toward stable and vibrant health. If you eat too much or too little (and that differs for different people at different times of the year), you will pay the inevitable price. It may not be today or even tomorrow, but we eventually reap the results of our dietary habits.

It isn't easy to eat well; it isn't always convenient. We therefore have to understand clearly how our dietary patterns can affect our lives. That clear look can provide motivational momentum to overcome inertia or self-indulgence.

Knowledge, however, is not a sufficient answer, evidenced by physicians and nutritional scientists who are in poor health from having eaten what they know they "shouldn't have."

We can sensitize ourselves over a period of time by paying attention to what we put into our mouths and how we feel afterward. Then we need to *act* upon our understanding.

In addition to diet, we also need to balance our habits of posture, breathing, and rest if we are to achieve optimum vitality. This vitality in turn gives us the power to develop our physical talent.

The Four Ss of Physical Talent

I have already discussed the mental and emotional components of what we call talent. In order to achieve high levels of skill, we also need to develop a full measure of physical qualities.

What we call *physical talent* is composed of four primary

qualities, each of which begin with the letter S: *strength, suppleness, stamina, and sensitivity.* When we call someone talented, we are usually noting that the person has a strong foundation based upon these four attributes.

Most learning blocks and frustrations we encounter on the athletic journey, particularly those related to skill-learning in sports, games, music, dance, or martial arts, are related to a lack in one or more of these four aspects of physical talent.

As we develop all four of these four key qualities, we actually raise our potential. We often call talented athletes "gifted," as if they were given their prowess as a birthday gift and are somehow "lucky." Most of us have probably heard the old saying, "I believe in luck—and I find that the harder I work, the more of it I have."

Although our genetic makeup—inherited body type, nervous system, and so forth—does contribute toward our overall potential, I believe that talent is far more developed than inborn. What we get at birth is at best a predisposition; what we do with it is up to us. I've seen many "gifted" athletes fall by the wayside because of lack of desire, interest, and direction. I've also seen many athletes that few people would call gifted go on to develop high levels of talent; in other words, they changed themselves from "slow learners" to "fast learners" by elevating their levels of strength, suppleness, stamina, and sensitivity.

Let's take a look at each of the four Ss to appreciate our current, and potential, levels of talent. Before we do, however, it's essential to look at the master key that unlocks all four of these fundamental building blocks.

Relaxation: The Master Key to Physical Talent

The less effort, the faster and more powerful you will be.
                    —*BRUCE LEE*

Relaxation enhances strength, suppleness, stamina, and sensitivity. By the end of this chapter, you'll understand how and why.

Studies of efficiency in movement carried out at several universities showed that people tend to use wasted effort and unnecessary muscular tension in even the simplest movements such as lifting a fork, holding a book, sitting in a chair. Not only did the subjects use more tension than necessary; they also tensed muscles that were unrelated to the movements being made.

Now, as you become acclimated to relaxation—a sense of ease in stillness and movement—you also begin to notice any chronic tension, and you have the power to release it. This represents a giant step on the path of the inner athlete.

Relaxation is the best single indicator of your whole-body well-being. Your degree of relaxation across the three centers—physical, metal, and emotional— precisely reflects your trust in and alignment with the natural laws. Physical ease is a mirror of the relationship of body to mind. When you are truly relaxed, centered, at ease, the mind comes to rest, the emotions flow clearly, and the vital body surrenders itself to nature's flow. All feels right with the world then, because all feels right with the body.

Like children, natural athletes are free from all inhibiting tension. They have come to recognize their tension and have learned to release it in the same moment. They therefore experience a deep storehouse of energy, sufficient to enjoy a simple life as well as to bounce through their athletic exploits.

> *Our ability to relax*
> *reflects our willingness to trust.*
> *—ANONYMOUS*

Most of us have carried subtle tensions for so many years

that we've forgotten what *real* relaxation is. Rather than a temporary state achieved by dissipating knotted energy; it is a *continual* enjoyment of muscular release *and* high energy at the same time.

It does little good for me to advise people to "relax" until they know what relaxation feels like and until they become aware of the degree of tension they carry.

―――――― **TESTING FOR RELAXATION** ――――――

Ask a friend to lift your arm as you endeavor to let it hang limp. Notice whether or not you unconsciously "help" your friend lift your arm, or whether your arm is totally dead weight. Do this experiment with a friend, and you'll notice how some people, as a result of chronic, unconscious, and energy-wasting tension they carry with them all day, cannot let their arms relax, try as they might.

As you learn to master this "letting go," it will help you maintain a sense of release throughout the day—and when you do become tense, you'll notice it more readily and can release the tension (TENSE-SHAKE-BREATHE-RELAX).

A relaxed arm should shake like jelly when someone takes your hand in both his or her hands and shakes vigorously. If your arm is lifted and released, it should drop to your side instantly. If you carry a lot of tension (as do many older people, having stored it over the years), the arm may even stay in place for a long moment before dropping.

If the preceding exercises helped you become aware of any chronic tension you carry, the following exercise will provide the means to release it, over time, by providing an experience of profound relaxation.

——— DEEP RELAXATION EXERCISE ———

Lying on your back on a carpet or mattress, loosen any tight clothing. Have a friend read the following instructions, or else record them and play them back. Once you know the steps and your body gets accustomed to this state, you can easily go through the process any time, even in a few minutes.

Be aware of the body's weight. Breathing slowly and naturally, surrender to gravity. Notice the floor pressing up against the body and the body pressing equally down into the floor.

Put your attention on your feet . . . imagine that they are very heavy. Feel the skin heavy, the bones heavy . . . the whole body becoming heavy. . . .

Feel the deep, profound heaviness spreading up into your lower legs and through the knees, releasing all the muscles. Feel the lower legs heavy . . . the skin heavy, the bones heavy . . . the whole body becoming heavy.

Feel the heaviness continue into the thighs and buttocks. Feel all the muscles of the thighs release and the buttocks relax, feel the skin heavy, the bones heavy . . . the whole body becoming heavy.

Let the pleasant heaviness sink deep into the lower back, releasing . . . and continue into the upper back, around and under the shoulder blades, along the spine . . . releasing . . . heavy. Let the muscles of the upper back and neck and shoulders sink into gravity's pull . . . skin heavy, bones heavy . . . the whole body heavy.

Let go of the upper arms . . . the elbows and lower arms . . . feel the heaviness all the way to the fingertips . . . skin, bones . . . the whole body . . . heavy.

Feel all the muscles of the neck . . . front, back,

and sides, release and sink to the floor . . . skin, bones . . . the whole body heavy.

Now the entire body below the neck is heavy, totally relaxed. If you feel any tension left any-where, let it go, and become twice as heavy.

Now, as I name the areas of the face and scalp, feel them as heavy, and let them go with gravity . . . skin, bones . . . the whole body . . . heavy . . .

Feel the scalp release . . . all the muscles of the forehead . . . around the eye sockets . . . the cheeks, letting go . . . the muscles around the nose . . . the mouth and jaw, all releasing . . . the chin, and around the ears.

Now your entire body is in deep relaxation. Energies flow through the body freely, revitalizing, healing, rebalancing.

Notice the breathing. Imagine you're floating gently, on your own warm, private ocean. On inhalation, feel yourself float slowly up, and on exhalation, float back down . . . feeling the well-being of total relaxation.

Imagine the blood coursing freely through the body, nourishing it. Feel the energy of the body, vibrating within the cells.

Feel the peacefulness of relaxation. Notice how calm the mind is in this moment—and how open the emotional feelings are. The next time you expe-rience any emotional upset, let the body relax into this pleasant state.

Imagine yourself walking, with this same feeling of release . . . using only the muscular effort you need, and no more. Feel the lightness and effort-lessness of running . . . or playing your favorite sport with the same relaxed grace. . . .

As you feel this state, know that you can return
to it at will. Now begin to increase the depth of
your breathing. Ending with three gigantic breaths
of energy, open your eyes, and sit up. Stretch like a
cat.

The consummate athletes and artists in every field have
attained an ease of movement through efficient use of muscles. Dynamic relaxation is the foundation of all physical talent. Let's see how, beginning with strength.

Strength

Nothing is so strong as real gentleness;
nothing is so gentle as real strength.
                    —*ANONYMOUS*

If we had no voluntary muscle tissue, we'd spend our
very brief life as a puddle of protoplasm, a heap of skin,
organs, and bones. People with muscular disabilities appreciate that which we take for granted: the ability to *move at
will.*

Now any physiologist will tell you that if you stimulate
enough muscle fibers for a given demand over a period of
time, the body will create larger fibers to meet the demand.
Muscular strength increases in proportion to the effort of
training. That all seems straightforward. Yet there's more to
muscle than meets the eye.

Anyone knows that strength is one of the primary qualities of physical talent. What many of us may not have considered, however, is how to *use* strength properly in balance with
relaxation. "Strength" is more than the ability to contract muscle tissue; strength is the overall ability to *control movement.*

A teammate of mine at the University of California could

easily press himself up to a handstand from a prone position—flat on his belly on the floor. (To appreciate this, you might lie down on your belly and imagine just bending your arms as if to do a push-up, but trying to push your entire body right up to a handstand.) Brad was obviously well-muscled.

In order to accomplish this movement, Brad primarily used triceps (extensor) muscles. He could accomplish this movement over and over in practice. In competition, however, when he usually became tense, he unconsciously tightened *too many* muscles. Instead of just using his extensor muscles, he also tensed his biceps (flexor) muscles. These antagonistic muscle groups "fought" one another, resulting in a standoff and exhaustion. When nervous or trying too hard, Brad couldn't push up to the handstand. It wasn't a matter of strength—he had the muscles—it was a matter of control.

To one degree or another, this happens to each of us.

In order to use his strength, Brad had to practice not more strength but selective relaxation of unnecessary muscles. Many athletes who train intensively for strength, developing large, powerful muscles, may nevertheless have diminished *effective strength* because they are generally tense and haven't "educated" their appropriate muscle groups in complementary tension-relaxation. They therefore can't hit or throw as hard, run as fast, leap as high, or react as quickly as they might.

Since effective strength is the ability to relax the proper muscle groups while consciously tensing others, it may come as no surprise to you that babies have this ability. Put your finger in a baby's grasp, and try to pull away. Those little hands are surprisingly relaxed—and surprisingly powerful.

> *Greatness lies not in being strong*
> *but in the right use of strength.*
> *—ANONYMOUS*

One study compared the movement abilities of six month-old babies and some professional football players. The athletes tried to copy every movement and posture of these babies for ten minutes without stopping. Not a single athlete could keep up; they all dropped out from exhaustion within a few minutes.

Body-builders may appear the strongest in terms of weight they can lift, but in the economies of strength, women gymnasts, who have far less muscle tissue, are excellent examples of effective strength in action. And look at the cat! You won't see any muscle-bound cats walking around, yet what athlete can match a cat's movement abilities? I've seen cats jump ten feet straight up from a sitting position. A cat can be napping, then instantly spring after a mouse with blinding speed, then, just as suddenly, stop and clean its paws, totally relaxed. The cat carries very little tension. You can squeeze its muscle to the bone, and it will show no pain. Try squeezing *your* calf muscles to the bone, and feel the tension.

Various exercise systems emphasize relaxation-in-movement as a primary objective. One system taught taught by the Arica Institute, called eurythmics, entails the gradual tensing and relaxing of different parts of the body to a regular rhythm while maintaining complete relaxation elsewhere. It's possible eventually to master the conscious tensing of twelve different parts of the body independently. Training like this is very useful before running out and pumping iron.

As in the other sections, I am not outlining many individual how-to exercises, because although you can learn *about* movement from a book, its is immensely difficult and usually inappropriate to learn from a book *how to* move. Everyone has individual needs. It's best to get individual feedback from a teacher.

There are, however, a few simple routines you can perform to experience relaxed strength. The first comes from Aikido. This exercise is done with a partner, who will gradually try to bend your arm twice—the first time against your resistance, the second time against your nonresistance.

UNBENDABLE ARM

Test 1. Hold your right arm out in front of you, first clenched, arm *slightly* bent, with your wrist on your partner's shoulder. Your partner puts one hand on the crook of your elbow and gradually begins to push down, in order to bend your arm (in the direction it normally bends, of course). You resist, tensing your arm.

Shake your arm loose before Test 2.

Test 2. Standing balanced, place your wrist on your partner's shoulder as before, this time with your fingers extended and spread.

Your partner will again begin pushing downward gradually, as if to bend your arm.

This time, however, you'll remain free of tension. Let your arm be totally relaxed, yet strong—not like a wet noodle. You do this by imagining a powerful flow of energy, like water gushing through a hose, continually flowing through your arm and out the ends of your extended fingers, shooting right through the wall for a thousand miles.

Let your awareness "flow" with the energy and not stop at your partner's arm. As your partner begins to push more, imagine an increase in the power of the flow, balancing the pressure.

Experiment with this, and see if you begin to feel a new kind of strength, free of tension.

For those accustomed to this kind of strength, the arm becomes nearly unbendable when relaxed and actually much "weaker" when tensed. It works not because of a magical energy flow but because you are using only the amount of muscle tissue you actually need. This develops not only great effective strength but a feeling of ease.

Now, if you like, you can do another simple exercise that highlights the way mental attitude can influence effective strength.

In this exercise, you will do two push-ups with tension and two free of tension.

1. Beginning from an up position, do two push-ups at a slow-to-moderate pace, with *every* muscle in your body *tensed*. This is what it's like to *try*. Clench your teeth, tighten your thighs, buttocks, stomach, neck . . . it's exhausting, and makes the push-ups seem difficult, right?

To a lesser extent, this is what most athletes do during training, since few athletes have practiced conscious relaxation-in-movement.

2. For the second two push-ups, imagine that you're a puppet on a string, suspended from the arms of a giant who is standing directly over you. The giant will do work for you. Starting from the same up position, just relax down effortlessly, and imagine the giant pulling you up on the strings. Let the push-up happen by itself.

By sustaining and acting upon the image of energy flow or movement happening by itself, you create the psychophysical effect of relaxed strength, and all three centers—

physical, mental, and emotional—tend to harmonize in their natural relationship.

Strength cannot be free to work unless balanced with relaxation. The height you can jump from a standing position is a factor both in your ability to relax and in your ability to then push and spring. Try standing up, crouching down a bit, tensing your legs as hard as you can ... then jumping. You can hardly move.

Dale was captain of the Stanford gymnastics team. He was a floor-exercise and tumbling specialist. He was one of the hardest workers on the team. Each day, Dale would begin with calisthenics, then squat jumps for leg strength; he ran about three miles every day; he practiced his tumbling sequences over and over and over. His legs were well-muscled and his diet excellent. He was slim, yet his tumbling made him look as though he weighed 500 pounds; he just couldn't seem to get up into the air. A few beginning tumblers with legs like toothpicks would run out and tumble higher than he could. It used to drive him crazy.

Dale had plenty of muscle but too much tension. Muscle weighs more than fat. There is a point, especially for someone who *must move his own body* rapidly and lightly, at which development becomes over-development. In order to get stronger, Dale could have spent an entire summer without a single strength drill and just practiced relaxation. His tumbling would have made a sudden improvement.

Through accommodation, your muscles will develop in response to a demand. Balance that demand between sheer power and the ability to be loose and relaxed. That way, you'll develop full *use* of your muscles, not just "full power."

Once you develop your capacity for *relaxed power*, your movements will take on a new quality of effortlessness and grace, leading to improved speed, coordination, reflexes, and real response-ability—in the gym, on the field, and throughout daily life.

Suppleness

To most of us, suppleness implies stretching exercises. This may for the most part be true. Yet a baby needs no stretching exercises because it carries no tension—and neither did you, a long time ago. As you grew, however, you began to activate habitual tensing of muscles in response to physical pain, psychological threat, or emotional upset. You began to store unresolved upsets over the years, in the form of tension (just as the body stores nonutilized energy in the form of fat). Your body therefore became less naturally supple, and remedial exercises like stretching have become necessary.

Tension—leading to stiff joints, aches and pains, and decreased circulation, as well as contributing to arthritic conditions—is an unconscious, maladaptive strategy that we all have to become responsible for. That means noticing our stored tension and using appropriate measures to dissolve it.

The naturally supple body is a reflection of a relaxed mind. I'm not suggesting, however, that you start psychoanalysis to undo all past trauma in order to find some peace and flexibility. Just remember to notice tension in the course of your daily life—perhaps in the thighs, neck, back, face, or gut. Notice when you begin to tense; then relax. Do this more and more. You may never be inclined to invest large amounts of time and energy researching the causes of all those childhood upsets, but you can be responsible for tension *in this moment.*

Yes, stretching *is* a remedial activity—but a remedial activity that most of us need. Once you recognize that mental and emotional tension imposed upon the body is the source of your relative degree of stiffness, you can naturally form the right approach to stretching. You can avoid the usual method of needlessly inflicting even more pain and tension on yourself by improper stretching, by pushing (and pulling) too hard.

Stretching should be relaxed and intelligent, not just enthusiastic.

Most athletes push and pull their bodies through various extended positions either casually or aggressively, gritting their teeth in pain. The rest of the day they only tense up again and must repeat the same painful process. They'll probably feel some progress as the body adapts to the daily stretching, but this kind of program is a "two steps forward, one step back" approach. It's painful, and it sets up non-pleasurable psychological reactions.

The best recipe I know for suppleness is three parts relaxation to one part stretching. Without doing *any* stretching, you become more supple when you're relaxed, on vacation, or free from usual concerns. (On the other hand, many athletes become tighter, even while stretching, during exam times.)

If you "ask" your body to grow more supple, it will—*if* you ask it *nicely*. The following guidelines are "nice" ways to ask your body to stretch. Make a gentle demand, and you'll receive a positive response.

——— WHOLE BODY STRETCH ———

1. When it comes to your own body, you are a stretching expert. You don't need to seek the advice of others. You know more about precisely where, and to what degree, you need to stretch than any expert, for the body in question is *yours*.

Simply relax into a slightly more extended position than you're used to, whenever you feel tight. That sounds almost too simple, but that's all there is to it. You don't need to know anatomy. Just feel where you're tense—maybe it's the neck or lower back or behind the knees. If so, gently sit or bend just a little more. *Breathe deeply,* and imagine the breath going to the tight area, relaxing it.

Even you great athletic types should be as gentle with your bodies as if you were 98 years old.

2. Stretching should feel *good,* like a cat stretching after a nap. Balance between pleasure and pain.

3. Stretch only a little, but do it at least twice each day. It's better doing three or four minutes of relaxed stretching twice a day than fifteen minutes of grinding it out, once a day. Sneak up on it; remember to ask the body nicely . . . but ask it often.

4. Stretch when the body is warm. It's easier, it feels better, and it does you more good when you're warm. (Cold stretching hurts more, and you're more likely to be tense.)

5. Stretch any way you feel like it. I don't normally recommend bouncing vigorously, but a gentle pulsing bounce is okay if that feels good to you. If, however you sink into the stretch position for a few deep, relaxed, feel-good breaths, that may allow you to gain more benefits. *Experiment.*

6. Experimentation is the key. Find the most gentle, pleasurable way to stretch; it's only another of the body's games, after all. Later, you can develop more challenging stretches.

I present no specific stretching exercises here; the main thing is for you to determine the suppleness factors specific to your own activities and needs. What movements do you normally perform in training and daily life? Gradually make a demand to extend that range of motion.

Books, classes, or stretching with a friend are all helpful. Hatha yoga, T'ai Chi, Aikido, dance, or gymnastics, as well as the books, *Stretching,* by Bob Anderson, and *The Weekend Athlete's Way to a Pain-Free Monday,* by H. Jampol, will likely suit your needs.

Suppleness means a state of full articulation of all movable joints, including wrists, shoulders, neck, the entire spine, pelvis, hips, thighs, hamstrings, and ankles. The object of stretching is to open and free all joints, depending upon the demands of your favorite activities. If you become supple beyond the actual point of need, you'll feel an ease of movement. You'll also extend your range of power.

In general, suppleness should be given priority over strength—or at least developed prior to the major strength development—since the more supple you are, the less energy you need to expend in order to move the body. *Suppleness is the embodiment of nonresistance.*

Freedom from Lower Back Pain

Lower back pain often originates in mental or emotional stressors, such as starting a new business, or handling relationship conflicts. The four most common sources of lower back pain are:

1. weak abdominals
2. a stiff lower back
3. a weak lower back
4. tight hamstrings.

By strengthening the abdominals, stretching and strengthening the lower back, and stretching the hamstrings (at the back of the legs), most lower back pain is reduced or eliminated. Of course, massage and deep-tissue work as well as postural alignment work also help heal sore backs.

Suppleness, strength, and relaxation are intimately related. Movement requires all three if it is to become natural. If a joint is frozen, no amount of strength will move it. If you want to lift your leg high into the air to do a dance step, kick a football, or perform a gymnastics movement, you need both strength (to lift the leg) and suppleness (to allow the full range of motion through which the muscles work). Effective movement always requires the integration and balance of suppleness and strength.

Suppleness—developed through awareness of tension, conscious relaxation, and proper stretching—will improve your game and decrease muscle pulls, sprains, and related injuries. It will increase the muscle's responsiveness through increased blood flow.. You'll feel more awake and alive in daily life as your range of movement increases. You'll literally feel younger again. You can be as supple as a gymnast or dancer.

If you relax, you'll become supple. As you increase your suppleness, you'll also tend to become more naturally relaxed. In your relaxation, you'll begin to notice another change—and that change is our next topic.

Sensitivity

A legendary master of t'ai chi was so sensitive to the forces around him that if a fly landed on his shoulder, he would sway gently, under its "impact." A sparrow was unable to jump from his open palm and fly, because as it pushed away, his hand would sink beneath its legs. We all enjoy hearing stories about such people, who seem to possess "supernatural" attributes or abilities. Yet the description of this t'ai chi master reflects only natural abilities refined to a high degree through practice.

Sensitivity just means enhancement of senses and can refer to sight, hearing, taste, and so on. Most relevant for athletes are the sensory receptors and kinesthetic senses that enable them to move effectively. These senses include the following: balance, the vertical reflex, or ability to detect subtle divergence from the vertical, and to correct for it; *coordination*, the ability to move different parts of the body independently, with different degrees of muscular contraction, or to deliberately unify all the parts around a central axis of movement; *timing* and *rhythm*, the ability to start or stop a given movement at the correct moment; and *reflex speed*, the ability to respond quickly to a given stimulus.

You might expect someone with excellent coordination to have good timing and rhythm as well, along with superior balance and fast reflexes. And you would be right. Balance, coordination, timing, rhythm, and reflex speed are all interrelated; they are only different manifestations of neuromuscular *sensitivity*. As you develop great sensitivity, *many* attributes will shine.

If you concentrate on one aspect of sensitivity, such as balance, the other aspects will also develop. That is one reason it's wise to expose yourself to a variety of movement activities. The proficient *tennis* player who, in order to improve his tennis, takes a beginning gymnastics or dance or hatha yoga class (which place greater demand on the refinements of balance, suppleness, and relaxation) is a wise athlete.

Beyond what has already been outlined, you don't have to do anything to achieve greater sensitivity, for it will come with recognition of tension and relaxing: it's a natural result of stretching gently, of "asking nicely" for greater range of motion each day.

Sensitivity enables you to learn more rapidly and with greater ease, because your body picks up cues faster. As you become more sensitive you feel errors more quickly and correct them with greater consistency. You copy the experts better, because you open the circuits between your eyes and your muscular feedback. You cut through old, maladaptive compensations more easily, because you won't be as deeply locked into patterns of tension.

You've learned that you first have to recognize an error before you can correct it. Try this experiment:

Test 1. Look around you and find two objects nearby of different weight, such as a paperweight and a pencil.

What you're going to do is pick up one object and put it down, then pick up the other object and put it down—sensing the difference in weight.

Test 2. Pick the objects up, one after the other, but let your arm be relaxed. See how easy it is to sense the difference in weight.

There are a number of reasons you were able to sense the weight difference of the two objects more easily when relaxed, but they aren't important here. The main purpose of the exercise is to show how tension can limit your sensitivity. On more subtle levels, even a small amount of tension interferes with a refined sense of balance, timing, coordination, reflex speed. The natural athlete is a paragon of apparent contrasts, capable of unleashing awesome power, yet so soft, smooth, and sensitive that he can pick up on the most subtle cues. As your natural training progresses, you'll dissolve even the subtle blocks to learning.

The primary message of this section so far is that it takes more than running out and playing blindly to develop a foundation of natural physical talent. First, a natural order of training must be reestablished, with intelligent priorities. That's why I emphasize relaxation above all else. *Then* it's possible to develop strength properly without waste of energy. Free of unnecessary tension, you can develop suppleness more effectively. All these attributes serve as a foundation of sensitivity, and everything else falls into place.

Nevertheless, learning skills requires practice, and practice requires stamina. We now turn to stamina and its role in physical talent.

Stamina

The most proficient athletes spend a lot of time playing and practicing. No athlete ever became an expert without investing time and energy. Thus, in its own way, stamina—or the ability to work over a period of time—is a vital aspect of physical talent.

Stamina is a perfect reflection of the law of accommodation—that a demand over a period of time creates a specific development. It takes stamina to perform any action over an extended period of time. Writing a book, for example, requires a kind of stamina different from running a marathon. Anyone caught in rush-hour traffic or long lines at the bank knows that there are mental and emotional kinds of stamina, too. Since this section deals with physical talent, however, I will focus on physical stamina or endurance.

If you place a demand on your lungs and heart to bring oxygen to the tissues more rapidly, they'll accommodate. If you make a demand on your muscles to work for longer periods of time, they'll adapt to that demand. The principle of aerobic development works on this principle. Aerobic capacity is an accurate measure of stamina.

Stamina is a natural response to training; therefore, it isn't necessary to spend time developing it before you begin training, In fact, that wouldn't even be desirable, since the best stamina for you is specific to the activity you choose. if you're a tennis player, it's better to play many fast rounds of tennis than to jog ten miles through the park.

Stamina is also a function of relaxation, strength, and suppleness. Natural athletes who have freed themselves from the burden of chronic tension will, in their relaxed state, require less effort to build stamina. Suppleness allows greater movement with less energy, because when an athlete is supple the joints are free of drag from constricted connective tissue. All athletes must develop stamina over periods of time, but the natural athletes are ahead when they begin.

It takes time to get into shape, but not as much time as some of us fear. Lawrence Morehouse, a UCLA researcher, and other colleagues have found that in six weeks of inactivity, we can lose 80 percent of our conditioning—and in six more weeks of progressive training, we can also regain 80 percent of our peak condition.

We don't have to hurt in order to develop stamina. The jogger who has trained for two weeks, running one and a half miles on level ground, and then decides to start running hills for three miles is forgetting natural order. Learn how to develop stamina *gradually*. You'll inevitably get to whatever level of fitness you want, depending upon how long you continue progressive training—*not* how fast you do so. "Getting in shape" can be a thoroughly invigorating, pleasurable activity. It will require some adjustments and even discomfort as your body adapts to an increased demand, but if it hurts a lot, you're "pushing the river."

Though the best training for stamina is *specific* practice of your sport, you can, during pre- or off-season, practice general endurance like strength training or aerobic activities. If you do, you will be able to start regular training without exhaustion, aches and pains, or injury during your first days of enthusiasm.

How to Avoid Athletic Injuries

Injuries are the plague of athletes. The pain involved is the *least* of it. A single injury, whether developed over a period of time or all of a sudden, can undo all the time and energy of training and may end a career permanently. Injuries inevitably leave a trace of tension and fear in the body. They're a traumatic setback and never seem to happen at a convenient time. Injury is the negation of the primary purpose of sport—health and well-being.

Injury is most often the result of fundamental weakness in a mental, emotional, or physical aspect of talent (or a combination of these). "Accidents" aren't really accidents. If we injure ourselves, or if someone else injures us, *someone* wasn't paying attention, was upset, or wasn't physically prepared. In fact, these three variables—attention, upset, and lack of preparation—account for all "accidents" in daily life that can be linked to human error.

To avoid "accidents," therefore, we need to develop mental clarity and attention, emotional stability (and abiding motivation), and physical preparation. They are the three best insurance policies you'll ever have—and they don't cost a cent.

Acute injury, resulting from an impact (a fall, a collision, a blow) or from another force (such as a torque or twist) that is beyond the body's limits of tolerance is actually much more rare than *chronic* injuries, or those developed over periods of time through improper training or insufficient preparation. Natural training helps eliminate both kinds of injury by undermining the causes of them.

In order to highlight for you some of the major causes of injury—mental, emotional, and physical—I'm going to create a patsy, a "fall-guy" named Jerry.

Jerry sprained his ankle and couldn't understand how this "accident" happened to him.

Mental factors. Jerry is distracted very easily, either by his own thoughts or by activities going on around him. He thinks of himself as being a "klutzy guy." He has a habit of criticizing himself mercilessly and harbors latent tendencies to punish himself through pain. He has serious conflicts about competing, and the season is about to begin.

Emotional factors. Jerry's motivation to play rises and falls. Sometimes he's really "fired up," but other times he wishes he were on the sidelines. He's always been afraid of contact sport and any risky maneuvers, so he tenses up at the wrong times. Sometimes he hangs back and hesitates. Sometimes he gets angry and stomps around the gym, paying no attention to what's going on.

Physical factors. Jerry's ankles are stiff and relatively weak. Because of general tension, he's insensitive to fatigue and on some days pushes himself too far; he's overweight and in poor general condition.

Jerry should be glad he only sprained his ankle.

Looking back on the few injuries I've inflicted on myself in the athletic arena, I see the reasons clearly now and have been able to avoid further trauma since. How many of us "knew but didn't do." We knew we shouldn't lift a heavy object like that, but we did. We knew we shouldn't have played when we were tired or distracted, but we did.

Experienced inner athletes are attuned to their bodies' needs; injuries are, therefore, extremely rare in their training. They fully recognize injury as the price of insensitivity and inattention.

Mind-Body Balance

A chain breaks at its weakest link,
and so do we.
                        —ANONYMOUS

I've now surveyed the meaning of talent and the way it can be developed across the three centers of mind, emotions, and movement. When I first came upon this whole-body approach to athletic training, I was astonished to realize that paying attention to something like breathing could open the way to better balance or greater effective strength, because of the breath's influence on body and mind and emotions. Yet it works.

The following exercise shows how the mind can help the body to be centered and grounded.

————— **CONNECTION TO THE EARTH** —————

Tense Stand stiffly, breathing in the upper chest, with shoulders raised. Feel the tension. If any problem is bothering you, think about it.

Have a friend—say it's a woman—standing in

front of you reach under your armpits with her hands and lift you an inch or two off the floor as you hold onto her arms with your hands. Remain stiff and tense with shallow breathing as she lifts you.

(It doesn't matter whether or not your friend is actually able to lift you at any time—as long as you both can feel the difference between the first and the next attempt.)

Centered Next, shake loose and relax. Relax your mind by feeling the breath pleasantly in your lower belly. Feel physically heavy and stable, like a lazy cat or a sleeping baby. Let your shoulders hang down. Imagine your entire lower body is hollow— and then filled with water.

Resting your arms on your friend's arms, ask her to lift you in the same way as before—slowly, without any sudden movements. If you maintain this relaxed, centered focus, lifting you will become very difficult, perhaps impossible. You feel rooted to the ground.

This "rooting to the ground" is what the ancient masters of T'ai Chi perfected, through attention to mind and body talent. No one could push them over; legend has it that their mastery of natural forces enabled them to effortlessly toss opponents into the air.

In closing this section, we examine the unified state.

Satori and the Inner Athlete

Satori is a word from the Japanese Zen tradition that points to a "sudden awakening" or insight into our fundamental nature. This insight is not the result of abstract mental concepts or ideas but rather a momentary, experiential fusing of body, mind, and emotions. We experience Satori:

- when the *mind* is free of internal distractions, focused on the present moment;

- when *emotional energies* flow freely, uninhibited, expressive, manifesting as motivation;

- when the *body* feels vital, relaxed, energized, and sensitive. The athlete, artist, and musician all experience this state in the moment of truth. You can, in fact, experience it right now, with the following exercise.

INSTANT SATORI

Take your keys, a piece of fruit, or any handy object, and go outside. Throw the object up into the air. Staying relaxed and easy, catch it. Be sure to catch it. Then come back inside, and continue reading this exercise.

Now consider the moment that object was in the air. At that moment you weren't thinking of what you'd have for dinner or what you did yesterday. You weren't thinking of anything else, either. You may have been attending to thoughts before you threw it or after you caught it, but during the throw, you were pure attention, reaching out, waiting for the object's descent. In that same moment your emotions were open, and your body was alert and vitalized—a moment of satori.

This state of mind-body integration, inner-outer harmony, feels good on every level; it's the state that athletes describe in glowing metaphors; it's the essence of dynamic meditation and the instinctive "reason" we enjoy sports; it's the inner target of Zen archers. And over time, it becomes the natural state of the inner athlete.

Satori is the heart of the moving experience, a taste of inner peace and inner power.

THREE

The Inner Athlete in Action

**Great works are performed,
not by strength,
but perseverance.**
        —SAMUEL JOHNSON

*All useful training techniques reflect natural law. The strong,
stable, lower-body foundation yet relaxed, sensitive upper bodies we see in both martial artists and ballet dancers reflect
nature's wisdom. Only the tree with strong roots and trunk
but flexible, yielding branches will stand up in a hurricane.*

*As we embody natural law through conscious practice, we
master technique without memorizing how-to books.
Although most coaches and teachers have an ample supply of
principles relevant to their specific fields, the most powerful
principles apply universally to any sport or movement form.*

*Chapter 7 shares powerful learning techniques based on
natural law.*

7 Training:
Tools for Transformation

**What counts is not
the number of hours you put in
but how much you put in those hours.**

—ANONYMOUS

In this chapter, I will share key principles to enhance and accelerate your learning. No matter what activity you practice, you'll be able to apply the following principles, perspectives, and practices to your activity.

Warmup and the Transitions of Life

Our lives are filled with cycles and with periods of transition. Our growth from infancy through childhood, adolescence, and adulthood required many transitions into increasingly advanced modes of behavior, responsibility, and understanding. Birth and death are the Great Transitions. Graduation from school, beginning a livelihood, getting married, raising children, and retiring are all lesser but typical examples of changes in our lives. Life itself consists of a series of changes, sometimes smooth and orderly, sometimes unexpected, minute to minute, day to day, year by year. Inner athletes need the capacity to recognize these periods of transition in training and in daily life.

Years ago, while working in a busy office, I used to snarl at my wife when I arrived home from work until I realized that all I needed was a fifteen-minute transition to decompress, slow down, and space out before I was ready to listen happily to her news of the day.

Most of our transitions are sudden or nonexistent. Adolescence is a transition that leaves most of us unprepared and traumatized. Many of us have difficulties with the transitions of getting up in the morning or going to bed at night. Our minds, emotions, and physical rhythms may still be adjusted to an earlier frequency as we begin a new activity requiring much slower or faster vibrations. No wonder we sometimes have difficulty coping with new situations.

Transitions are in-between periods. When we leave work and are driving home, we're in between. When golfers hit the ball and are walking down the fairway, they are in between. Learning to enjoy and make use of these in-between periods will even out our lives. Unless we have learned to appreciate the value of in-betweens, our lives consists of jerky motions, highs and lows, stops and starts—a series of shocks. We make conscious use of transitions by noticing when we're moving from one kind of activity to another which ones may require a different mental, emotional, or physical approach.

Instead of leaping out of bed in the morning, we may find it useful to set the alarm fifteen minutes earlier, giving ourselves time to glide into the kitchen, put on some water for herb tea, read a few minutes, look out the window and take some deep breaths, say hello to a new day. I start my day by sitting up with my eyes still closed, doing a few slow, deep breathing exercises, and drinking a glass of water before I get out of bed.

You may wish to include some light calisthenics or to walk around the block before breakfast as part of your morning transition. This is only a suggestion; the main point is to create transition rituals that work for you.

Nowhere is a transition ritual so crucial as in the world of athletics. We call it a warm-up; it serves as a buffer zone between the day's prior events and the moment of truth in the athletic arena. A proper warm-up serves to prepare us for the unique demands of sport and helps us avoid days when nothing seems to go right.

Most of us are familiar with a physical warm-up to get the muscles warm, stretch out, and prepare physically for the intensity of training. Relatively few athletes appreciate the importance of a concurrent mental and emotional warm-up.

Engaging in *mental warm-up* means determining a clear course of action for the day. You'll want to choose realistic goals, based upon the circumstances and your energy level that day. Mental warm-up involves turning your attention to the place of practice, leaving all the day's cares and concerns at the door. Finally, you'll want to cultivate the proper attitude of respect and gratitude—the right mental "set"—for your activity. This is the purpose behind the Japanese tradition of bowing upon entering and leaving the practice hall.

Just as a decathlete needs a similar transition between the pole vault and javelin throw, a gymnast requires a mental transition between two pieces of apparatus because of the different qualities of each. Even a ballroom dancer needs to make a shift between a waltz or a disco dance. Runners and swimmers cultivate a different approach to sprinting and distance events; golfers need different mental warm-ups for driving and putting. Mental warm-up provides the proper focus and energy for each activity.

Emotional warm-up might begin with a few deep, calming breaths. Then you can recall the initial excitement you first felt about your sport and form a few mental images (mental warm-up) that create heightened emotional energy. Choose your emotional goal—focus on what fires you up about training. Imagine yourself succeeding at your goals; picture yourself winning because of a good practice day. Feel how much you can gain from some wisely directed energy.

Mental and emotional warm-up might seem to be long and involved, but they can actually take place almost simultaneously, at the speed of thought. The whole process might take place in the space of five slow, deep breaths or a moment of quiet contemplation as you make your transition. Many athletes do something like this subconsciously. Inner athletes do it consciously and strategically in order to control and amplify their direction and energy for the day.

Physical warm-up should be a definite period, set aside especially for the purpose. It doesn't have to (and probably shouldn't) be a long, involved process. Yet it is a time to get the body literally *warm*, oxygenated, fully awake, free of sluggishness—energized and relaxed. Never rush into warm-up— it's not the main event. Our bodies are like automobiles. You wouldn't want to start a cold engine, then race off at top speed. The oil (or, in our case, blood) isn't warm and flowing yet.

You may start some days feeling clogged up or lethargic. Don't let that discourage you. Some of my all-time best workouts began like that and ended well. It just took the body longer to warm up on that kind of day.

After a training session, you may wish to do some stretching and deep breathing exercises as a *warm-down*.

Learning How to Learn

When you were a child you may have had the opportunity to play in an empty lot, just after a fresh snowfall when the bare earth was hidden by a smooth cover of snow. Maybe that winter you were the first kid on your block to blaze that first straight, clean pathway through the crunchy, knee-deep carpet of white.

As it happens, the neurological pathways you blaze

when you learn a new movement pattern are just like the paths through that snowy field. The white carpet is your nervous system; the pathway is a neural one, and it represents a specific movement pattern or skill.

After all your preparation is done, you are ready to learn your new skill—blaze the correct neural pathway. Repetition of this pathway will lead to development of your skill. This applies to any movement pattern, simple or complex, whether running, jumping, swinging a bat, throwing a ball, or turning a triple somersault.

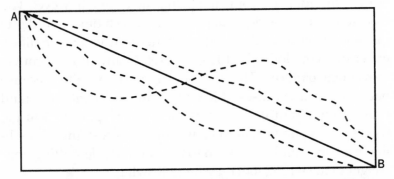

I use the image of the snow-covered lot (above) because it represents graphically what happens in your neuromuscular system when you are learning a new skill. The solid line from A to B shows the perfect execution of a skill. If line A—B is your first attempt at the skill, it means that you were totally prepared—mentally, emotionally, and physically—and were thus ready to perform it correctly the very first time.

Because most of us are not perfectly prepared, our first attempts are represented by the curving dotted lines above. Then we gradually home in on line A—B. This homing in process takes varying amounts of time, depending upon the approach to learning.

Your first attempt at a new skill is the most important one, because you've formed no previous pathway. The next time . . . and the next time, you're likely to follow the first path you

made. Every time you take the same neural pathway, you'll stabilize and reinforce that motor response *whether it is correct or
not.*

*Every time you let yourself practice a movement incorrectly,
you're increasing your ability to do it wrong.* It follows that you
want to repeat the correct movement pattern as much as possible and to avoid, at all costs, repeating an incorrect pattern. A
fundamental rule of learning, therefore, is this: *Never repeat the
same error twice.*

We know that errors are a part of learning. You will make
errors. In order to avoid stabilizing the errors, however, you
have to make consciously *different* errors each time, in order to
move yourself toward the correct pattern. If you make different errors, you don't habituate yourself to any single incorrect
movement pattern. This is a very important point, because
one of the prime causes of slow learning is repetition of (and
thus habituation to) one incorrect motor response. You get
used to swinging the bat too low; you get accustomed to arch-
ing in a handstand; you begin to feel comfortable shifting your
weight to the wrong foot on your golf swing.

As you consciously make each attempt *different,* you're
simply exploring the many possibilities for error as you home
in slowly to the straight path, the correct way, without forming
bad habits.

Awareness and Practice

If you practice hitting a thousand golf balls every day but
really pay attention to only two hundred swings, then you're
wasting eight hundred swings a day—and in fact, those eight
hundred semiconscious swings may be doing you more harm
than good, because, as I just pointed out, you can form bad
pathways without noticing it—like walking through the empty
lot in your sleep.

Practice doesn't make perfect; only perfect practice makes per-

fect. Proper learning technique consists not only of attempting the correct pattern but avoiding the incorrect one. Remain fully aware in your mind and in your body of *every* attempt you make during practice. If you make an error, never just "do it again." Take a moment to be fully aware of *what went wrong;* if you don't know, you'll just repeat the error. Then make a determined attempt to do something different.

The Stages of Practice

Most of us assume that if we want to become skilled, we must practice the skill over and over, many times. This is not necessarily true. Most beginners tend to practice *too much* at first. If you're a beginner at a particular skill, you'll probably have a low level of "feeling awareness" at first. You don't exactly know what the skill, performed correctly, should feel like. Don't practice many repetitions, therefore, or you're likely to develop incorrect patterns. Instead, begin with a *few* repetitions, maintaining *intense concentration* and *real interest.* You may continue while concentration and interest are strong; but if you begin to repeat an error, or if real interest and attention start to fade—if your approach becomes casual—then stop, and come back to your practice later on. Practice is like gambling: you have to know when to quit. When you find that you can consistently repeat the correct pattern, only then should you begin to do many repetitions for endurance and stabilization.

Following this principle, I taught myself within a very short time to juggle three balls. I'd try each progression, beginning with one ball, then two, and finally three, only four or five times each day. Working for five minutes a day, within five days I taught myself to juggle three balls. It's very true that some people, by practicing for an hour or two, might learn to juggle three balls in *one* day. What I want to emphasize, however, is that the way I suggest, aligned with *natural order* and realistic psychological dynamics, will allow you to learn *correctly.* Many "fast learners" also pick up little compensations and poor habit patterns. They may learn the skill fast, but they don't necessarily learn it *right.* Take the time to learn it right, and you'll save time. There's a big difference between learning and learning correctly.

As you practice, stop for a moment between each two attempts. "Check yourself," take a deep breath, shake loose, and relax. Feel awareness tingling through your body, out to your fingertips and toes. Feel your connection to the earth. Then continue.

Learning, then, is not just a matter of casually (or fiercely) performing a motion over and over. That may build stamina and muscles, but it will not necessarily develop the straightest path to natural ability. What you require is a *strategy of training* that employs insight and concentration in place of mechanical repetition. The following techniques and principles make up that strategy of effective learning.

Overcompensation

Overcompensation is the single most valuable aid to rapid learning you're ever likely to come across. Here's why: When you're performing an incorrect movement pattern over a period of time, you're going to become comfortable with that pattern. Any changes—even toward the correct pattern—are going to feel "strange" because you're not used to them. *When you're wrong, what's right feels wrong.* Because of this principle, *corrections tend to be insufficient.* Your attempts tend to cluster around your old habit.

If, for example, you're learning to hit a baseball and have formed a habit of swinging too high, you'll tend to continue swinging high. Even if someone tells you to swing lower, you'll correct only a little bit, otherwise it will feel "all wrong." Maybe you'll swing a little lower than before, but your swing will still be too high.

Recognizing the law of balance, therefore, you have to

apply overcompensation to your practice and work *both sides* of the movement. You have to make a determined attempt to swing "much too low." When you attempt this, it's best if you actually swing under the ball. After working both sides—too high and too low—you'll know where the middle is. (Most likely, though, in trying to swing "too low," you'll connect with the ball.)

The principle of overcompensation—or working both sides—applies to elements of timing, balance, accuracy, and force in every possible sport or movement art. It works on the same natural gyroscopic principle that allows a guided missile to home in on target quickly, by moving from one side to the other, until it finds the middle. "Finding the middle" is what effective learning is all about.

——— FASTER LEARNING THROUGH ——— OVER-COMPENSATION

I'm going to assume that catching an object in front of you that you've thrown up behind your back is a new skill for you. Take a lemon or other unbreakable fruit. Toss it behind your back and up over your shoulder, catching it in front of you in the same hand. You can throw the object over the same or the opposite shoulder of the hand in which you hold the object. The main object here is to make conscious use of *overcompensation*. Work on one variable at a time. If you threw too far left, then on your next attempt throw too far right. If you then throw too far behind you, make sure you throw way in front of you. Then you'll find the middle.

Using this principle, you should be able to learn this tricky skill in just a few minutes. You can then apply the same technique to any endeavor. But like many other athletes, you may experience resistance to working both sides; it may seem like a "waste of time" to try to do something deliberately wrong. You may feel impatient just to do it right the next time and want to avoid another wrong attempt even on "the other side." If that's the case, I hope the reasons behind the strategy of overcompensation are now clear, making its time-saving usefulness obvious.

If you are incapable of working both sides because of insufficient strength, suppleness, or other qualities that would enable you to overcompensate, then it's back to basics. You need more preparation, or else you'll only ingrain the error more deeply.

If you feel acutely uncomfortable or even fearful of working both sides because it "feels too strange" (especially if you're engaged in a high-risk sport), that's normal. If you're a high diver and you keep under-throwing a dive, you may feel just a bit nervous about the prospect of overthrowing the same dive. Still, the principle applies; you can make use of it or not. If you wish to learn successfully and rapidly, *you have to be willing to work both sides.*

Ideomotor Action and Mental Practice

Your powers of imagination can help you enhance old skills and learn new ones. This is possible because of the interaction of mind and muscle. In the negative sense, turbulent thought can impose muscular tension, as you've seen. On the positive side, clear mental imagery can—even without actual movement—develop correct muscular responses. This principle can be demonstrated with a simple experiment:

──────── **MIND MOVING BODY** ────────

Tie a small weighted object (like a ring) to a six-inch length of thread or string. Let the object hang by the string, held by your thumb and first finger. Hold the string still, then begin to imagine that the ring is swinging back and forth, back and forth. Continue to imagine this, and watch what happens.

Next, while the ring swings back and forth, imagine that it is going in a circle instead; see the results.

This test demonstrates the phenomenon of *ideomotor action*—that for any image of movement there is a subtle, corresponding muscular impulse. If you relax the body and imagine yourself performing a movement correctly, the muscles respond. Ideomotor action is a key principle behind mental practice.

The value of mental practice is well established in research. One study of mental practice used a group of sixty beginning basketball players. The group was split into three groups of twenty each. The first group practiced shooting baskets from the free-throw line, attempting a specified number of shots in a specified time for a period of two weeks. The second group was asked to practice *mentally* in exactly the same fashion—imagining themselves shooting baskets. The third group performed unrelated activities during that same time period.

Everyone in each group was tested at the beginning of practice and again after the two-week period. As expected, the third group didn't improve. Those who practiced *mentally,* however, improved almost as much as those who trained physically.

The moral of that study is not, of course, that we should begin practicing from the living-room couch but that mental practice can be very useful as a supplement to physical practice. I gained a reputation as a "natural" when I competed on the University of California's gymnastics team, because I seemed to learn difficult movements "effortlessly" on on the first try. What my teammates didn't know was that I would dream about those moves the night before and perform them in my head all day before actually attempting them. When I finally executed the movement physically, it felt as if I'd done it many times already. This confidence helped me to overcome fear, too.

In some situations especially, mental practice has distinct advantages:

- It's absolutely *safe*—unless you mentally practice your golf swing while driving down the freeway.

- You can do it *anywhere*. Be careful with this, however. I once imagined myself doing a trampoline routine while sitting in a dull political-science lecture. As I practiced, my arms made waving gestures as I "twisted" and "somersaulted." The professor stopped his lecture, and all eight hundred people in the hall strained for a look at "the guy in the front row having a fit."

- There's no fear of failure in mental practice, because it can be free of error; you can perform brilliantly.

There are exceptions to this rule, too. One of my gymnasts at the University of California consistently fell off the balance beam. As surely as the sun rose, as regularly as Monday followed Sunday, she'd fall off. She fell on weekdays or weekends, rain or shine, in practice or competition, without discrimination.

One day, out of sheer desperation—for her safety and my peace of mind—I suggested that she try mental practice for a while. "Go through five or ten routines perfectly, in your head," I said, feeling that perhaps in this way she'd develop a good habit.

I busied myself with the other gymnasts until later, when I glanced over and saw her sitting there, brows knitted with concentration, eyes shut tight, whispering to herself, "Damn! Oops . . . oh, damn!"

Puzzled. I asked her what was the matter. She replied,

"Oh, nothing, Coach. It's just that I keep falling off."

- Another advantage of mental practice is that it's free. If you take those private lessons twice a week instead of three times, or an hour each day instead of two, you can spend the rest of your time practicing in your imagination. You really get your money's worth.

- Mental practice means that you are concentrating automatically, because concentration is part of mental effort. You can do casual physical practice by just letting your body go through the motions without real attention. Not so with mental practice. Because of this, it isn't as easy as it sounds. You have to develop your capacity for visualization, imagery, and concentration, but once you do, your efforts will reap rewards of learning.

You can use mental practice if you're ill or injured, or at odd moments during the day when there's nothing much to do. It beats thinking about your problems—and you can get a jump on your favorite opponents.

As you imagine yourself doing well in competition or practice, this visualization will also serve to dissolve any limiting self-concept, since your subconscious mind doesn't differentiate strongly between what you see or do and what you imagine vividly.

Athletes who improve faster than equally-prepared counterparts simply put in more mental practice time. When someone would ask me how I learned a particular gymnastics move, I'd joke, "Oh, I think about it a lot." Actually, of course, thinking about the movement was part of my practice.

Mental practice also explains the common phenomenon of athletes returning to a sport after a layoff only to find that their technique has improved. It also explains the occurence of big improvemnt in a skill on a Monday after an athlete had trouble with it on a Friday and took the weekend off. In just thinking about the movements, it's possible for you to improve, because you don't practice any errors. Mental practice is more efficient than physical practice.

The main requirement of mental practice is to stay entirely relaxed so that no other muscle tensions interfere with the proper response. While practicing mentally you can lie down, or you can sit quietly. Of course, you have to have some kind of "feel" for the movement before practicing it in your imagination. Once you know how it should feel, practice it repeatedly in your mind.

Slow-Motion Practice

Slow-motion practice, a key to reaching the highest levels of mastery, gives you the time to be aware of *every part* of a movement, whether it's a baseball or golf swing, a javelin toss, or a karate punch. When you perform an activity in slow motion you can sense such complex parts of the act as weight shift and coordination of body parts. Since most unconscious errors occur in the middle of a movement sequence, slowing the movement down can have surprising benefits in ease and speed of learning, because mistakes that were formerly hidden can become painfully obvious.

SLOW-MOTION EXPERIENCE

Test 1. Hold your right hand in front of your face, so that you are looking into your palm. Quickly move your right arm out to the side, turning your palm outward, and stop. Notice that you were aware of only the beginning and the end of that movement.

Test 2. Now repeat the same sequence, but this time move your arm and hand in slow motion—as slowly as you possibly can. Let it take a full minute. Be aware of the relaxation of the arm and hand muscles. Notice how each finger turns; clearly see the different angles of your hand, as if for the first time.

In this test, you were clearly aware of the movement of your arm and hand in its entirety, from beginning to end. I discovered, after a period of slow-motion practice, that I could move faster than ever because in moving slowly I became aware of tension and was able to let it go. Without tension, it's possible to move with blinding speed.

Slow-motion practice is like studying slow-motion instant-replay films of training, except that in practice you're also *feeling*, not just seeing. You can apply this technique to virtually every sport or movement form. It applies particularly well to activities like golf, baseball, tennis, and handball. In coaching gymnastics, I often carry athletes slowly through a somersaulting movement so that they can become aware of every part of turning over. Slowing down your practice expands your awareness and eliminates the blurred blind spot encountered in rapid movements. You can be very creative in applying slow motion to different activities. (If you figure out how to apply it to skydiving, of course, I'd like to hear about it.)

Slow motion *works*, and it's fun. Like the practitioners of T'ai Chi, you may even discover that slow-motion sport is a form of moving meditation.

The Beginning-and-End Method

Beginning and end points are keys to a complete movement skill. Sometimes it isn't practical to work in slow motion—for example, in learning a cartwheel or a somersault. In cases like this, it's useful to pay strict attention to a perfect beginning and ending position. You may not have any idea where you are in the middle, but if the beginning and ending positions are just right, *the middle will take care of itself.* That's why so many coaches instinctively emphasize the correct follow-through.

Golf in particular benefits by awareness of the follow-through. Don't just swing the golf club, hit the ball, and move on. Hold the ending for a moment, and check your position, your balance, the position of your arms, head, and body. When I teach golf, the first emphasis is on balance and whole-body centering: then I show the best beginning and ending positions. These things form the basis of a consistent swing.

The physical application of beginning-end awareness is that if you complete a movement and find that you're in the wrong ending position—for example, if, in attempting a somersault, you find yourself ending up on your nose instead of your feet—you should move as rapidly as possible to the correct ending position. The next time, you'll find that you won't be quite as far off—perhaps on your ear this time—and you should again move instantly to the correct ending. Before long, you'll simply end in the proper position, and the middle will begin to flow smoothly as well.

Part-Whole Practice

Any skill, like the functioning of your car's carburetor, is made up of component parts. If you want to clean a carburetor and find out why it isn't working well, you take it apart and find the trouble spot. It works the same for a movement skill. The entire carburetor—or the skill—may be fundamentally all right . . . except for one little part (which can cause imbalance in the whole), but you don't know where it is. That's when analysis comes in very handy.

A good teacher or insightful student can dive to the source of the problem, undistracted by symptoms. Once isolated, the problem is practically solved.

I've found it useful to teach a new movement skill by breaking it down into its parts—first the beginning, then the middle, then the end. Afterward, it's easy to put the whole thing together.

Analysis can also be applied to specific drills that can save time and make learning an entire movement pattern much easier. Instead of isolating your practice to a single activity or skill, it's valuable to practice related drills. Divers, for example, will often train on the trampoline to learn somersaults and twisting without getting wet. Acrobatic skiers will do the same, because they can practice more repetitions with less energy. Pole vaulters can use certain gymnastics drills to learn more efficient ways of working the pole. These fundamental drills, which can be created and applied to any activity, save time.

The Programming Principle

Today, more and more *programmed instruction* is becoming available. It's possible to learn complex subjects—such as the fundamentals of law, medical terminology, English grammar, languages—through programmed material. Programmed video training for movement activities will soon become plentiful. Programmed learning is based on the principles that:

- we learn in *small steps,* taking it in simple and progressive increments.

- we take an *active part*—responding to the cues.

- we get immediate reinforcement and feedback—the correct answer is displayed as soon as we make our response.

- we feel successful, because of the small, simple progressions.

Good programmed learning is designed around commonsense principles. They make learning easy and therefore fun. I have approached learning—and teaching—using the same principles, and have found them to be of great use to myself and to my students. Any movement can be learned by first taking it apart (analysis), then practicing it in very simple progressions or steps. Programmed progressions allow for a *constant feeling of success* in which the *process of learning*—rather than a single end result—becomes the goal.

Imitation: The Ultimate Technique

Children are masters of imitation, the most powerful and natural way to learn. As infants, we were masters of imitation; it's how we learned to walk, talk, and use many other practical life skills; that is, before we learned that it was "bad" to be a "copycat," that we were supposed to do our "*own* work." I was fortunate enough to have parents who never discouraged my interest in imitation. They told me that it was fine to copy people as long as I was certain their qualities were worth copying. I extend that advice to you.

We can learn far more than athletic skills through imitation. As a young man, I modeled different personal "styles" by imitating the qualities I admired in people. Modeling these styles permitted me to "try on" different ways of being. I've never met a single person who didn't have at least one quality I admired.

Everything and everybody has a mixture of virtues as well as issues. If you look for the good in everyone you meet, that person becomes your teacher.

> *We have no friends;*
> *we have no enemies;*
> *we have only teachers.*
> —ANONYMOUS

To learn a skill, we need to find someone who is skillful

and watch that person carefully. Study the skilled person's musculature and movements, facial expressions, arms, and legs. As we watch such persons perform, we need to feel ourself moving in the same manner.

Our ability will improve with practice. Even the most creative painters began by copying. If you wish to copy a drawing of an accomplished artist, you may not be able to reproduce it precisely at first, but with practice, your copying will improve. We can practice copying anywhere or anytime.

Of course, in order to copy well we must first be *prepared;* we can't imitate a power-lifter unless we've developed some strength or imitate a ballet dancer unless we've developed the necessary suppleness and muscular control.

I'm convinced that imitation is the master technique of learning because it works at the subconscious level—as if one body learned directly from another without intervention of the intellect.

If you haven't made the best use of your innate powers of imitation, it's probably due to one of the following reasons:

- You may *not be sufficiently prepared to copy well.* (If so, back to basics; develop your talent.)

- You may experience *unconscious resistance* to copying someone else because of a belief that you must "live your own life" or because you feel that you could never imitate an expert's skill level (as a result of your low self-concept) or because you aren't ready to acknowledge that someone else may have a quality you don't presently possess. If the latter is the case, swallow your pride.

- You may be copying the wrong people or the wrong qualities. This is an ever-present fear of parents, who feel that their children may "pick up" the wrong qualities if their kids don't have proper playmates. Exposure does have a lot to do with the develop as a child and as an adult, since we don't imitate that which we've never seen.

―――――――― **IMITATION PRACTICE** ――――――――

Have a friend face you. Lets say your friend is a man. You hold his arm in an unusual position. Copy his arm position, as if looking in a mirror. Have him take another position, perhaps with both arms askew. Imitate that. Then mirror his posture. Do the same thing as he moves very slowly.

You'll find that, with a little practice, you can mirror your friend with a high degree of precision, and you can apply your ability to imitate in your sports activities and your daily life.

―――――――――――――――――――――――――――――――――

In this chapter I've outlined practical ways to learn how to learn. Only you have the power to bring the words and concepts to life. Start with the principles that make the most sense to you or that you find the most fun. If you use even a single one of these techniques to its fullest extent, it will enhance your game and can enrich your life.

Just do your best;
it's all you can do.
Don't ask how;
just begin,
and do it now.
The world waits for you.
        —*HAROLD WHALEY*

8 Competition: The Moment of Truth

**It may be that the race is not always to the swift,
nor the battle to the strong,
but that's the way to bet.**

—DAMON RUNYAN

In the living room, restaurant, or locker room, when the subject of competition comes up, there seem to be three dominant views: One group of us admires the competitive ethic as a Great American Tradition—"it's what made this country strong"—along with capitalism and the credo of the individual spirit. Another group, philosophically inclined to "peaceful coexistence, harmony, and cooperation," avoids competition as dehumanizing. This group prefers cooperative endeavors exclusively and gravitates instead toward New Games, looking to the East for inspiration. The third group doesn't much care either way.

Competition can bring out our best and worst, developing our strengths and revealing our weaknesses. Competition is one way to face a genuine Moment of Truth, of romance and adventure. Drawing the best from a man or woman, competition can be a model for positive, assertive, and realistic efforts

135

in daily life. Athletes tend to be successful because they know that life doesn't just hand you everything. Sports can, therefore, be a source of valuable life lessons for young people.

The competitive experience can, at its best, become a form of moving meditation in which all our attention, free of random daydreaming, is focused on the present moment. It's also an enjoyable form of entertainment for millions of people as well as a source of inspiration to many boys and girls.

Most athletes appreciate competition but are so steeped in it that they fail to recognize its "shadow side." In order to balance this picture, I'm going to spend more time exploring the problems of the competitive mind.

Competition compares unique human beings in specialized arenas, translating the whole of their efforts into scores, times, and measurements. Competition reinforces these polarized words—"winner" and "loser"—as if the world were divided into two camps dependent on athletic prowess. Children who play highly competitive games emerge as losers more often than winners, in spite of all our well-intentioned slogans about "it's how you play the game. . . ."

Competition tends to breed camaraderie among teammates but enmity for opponents. Before collegiate football games, I used to see pictures of the opposing team posted outside the training-room doors, with the words, "The Enemy" written below. Such a practice tends to encourage hostility in daily life, as evidenced by the way drivers treat one another as well as pedestrians. At some competitive events I've even seen athletes laugh or cheer when a member of the opposing team falls.

> *When I played pro football,*
> *I never set out to hurt anyone deliberately—*
> *unless it was, you know, important,*
> *like a league game or something.*
> *—DICK BUTKUS*

Competition may reinforce a simplistic, black-and-white way of thinking and looking at the world, with winning as the only valued goal, comparing ourselves to others in order to determine our own relative worth. Day-to-day improvement is probably a more meaningful measure of achievement than who beats whom, but the most improved players rarely receive the recognition or glory.

> *The Way of the sage is to act but not to compete.*
> —*LAO TZU*

A good example of competition as instilled by our culture in childhood is illustrated by the game of musical chairs. In his book, *No Contest: The Case Against Competition* (Houghton Mifflin), psychologist Alfie Kohn points out that in musical chairs, every round eliminates a child until at the end "only one child is left triumphantly seated while everyone else is standing on the sidelines, excluded from play. This is one way we learn to have a good time in America."

Most of us have played this game; few of us were traumatized by not finding a chair, but we remember the sinking feeling. Sure, life is tough, and we have to learn to deal with disappointment, with losing out sometimes. But what message did that innocent little children's game tell us? That there isn't enough to go around, so we had better scramble, maybe even push someone else aside, because we're either going to be "in" or "out." Games are invented within a society and reflect that society's needs and lessons.

Kohn pointed out that we may have to create other games to meet the needs of future generations. *No Contest* is a game based on the findings of several hundred studies that showed how competition undermines self-esteem, poisons relationships, and keeps us from doing our best—a particularly unsettling line of inquiry for athletes or parents. Most of us, after all, assume that competitive sports teach all sorts of useful lessons and, indeed, that games by definition must produce a winner and a loser. But I've come to believe with Kohn that recreation at its best does not require people to try to triumph over others. Quite the contrary.

Terry Orlick, a sports psychologist at the University of Ottowa, took a look at musical chairs and proposed that we keep the basic format of removing chairs but change the goal: instead, the children try to fit everyone on a diminishing number of seats. At the end, a group of giggling children tries to figure out how to squish onto a single chair. Everyone plays to the end; *everyone* has a good time.

Orlick and others have devised or collected hundreds of such games for both children and adults. The underlying theory is simple: All games involve achieving a goal despite the presence of an obstacle, *but nowhere is it written that the obstacle has to be someone else.* The purpose of a game can be for each person on the field to make a specified contribution to the goal, or for all players to reach a certain score, or for all to work with their partners against a time limit.

Note that in such games, an opponent becomes a partner. *In these activities the entire dynamic of the game shifts, and one's attitude toward the other players changes with it.*

Kohn might be encouraged by the game of "Effortless Tennis" originated by Brent Zeller, a gifted teacher who takes his students through a natural, flowing, non-stressful, and cooperative approach in which the goal is to keep the ball in play as long as possible by hitting it to where one's partner can return it.

Kohn believes that "not a single one of the advantages attributed to sports actually requires competition." Running, climbing, biking, swimming, aerobics—he points out—all offer a fine workout without any need to try and outdo someone else. Some people point to the camaraderie that results from teamwork, he says, but that's precisely the benefit of cooperative activity, the very essence of which is that *everyone* on the field is working together for a common goal. The distinguishing feature of team competition, by contrast, is that a given player works with and is encouraged to feel warmly toward only half of those present.

Kohn also questions our dependence on sports to provide a sense of accomplishment or to test our wits. "One can," he points out, "aim instead at an objective standard (How far did I throw? How many miles did we cover?) or attempt to do better than last week. Such individual and group striving—like cooperative games—provides satisfaction and challenge without competition."

Kohn's essay asserts: "Studies have shown that feelings of self-worth become dependent on external sources of evaluation as a result of competition; your value is defined by what you've done and who you've beaten."

Competition, he says, also hurts our relationships with each other because "each child inevitably comes to regard others as obstacles to his or her own success. Competition leads children to envy winners, to dismiss losers . . . and to be suspicious of just about everyone."

Kohn's views are thought-provoking and represent a new, evolutionary alternative in the way we conduct human affairs, as individuals, groups, and nations.

Some activities, such as boxing and other martial arts, as well as combative games like football, ice hockey, and the like, tend to engender aggressive competitive feelings. In other sports activities, such as swimming, track and field, and certainly gymnastics, athletes may not see others as enemies or adversaries at all; rather, they may focus on how fast they were able to perform. And the highest quality athletes take no comfort or pleasure in winning a contest because their competitor was ill that day or performed poorly—especially if they themselves "won" while turning in a lackluster performance.

In the animal kingdom, Darwinian survival of the fittest,

the ultimate competition for prey, for food, still prevails. It could be argued, perhaps, that competition is thus "natural" to us, and arguments against it are unrealistic, idealistic, or impractical. But if we view ourselves only as other animals, no different from the beasts of prey, we can never rise above them. Humans have the ability to rise above biological tendencies, individually and as a species.

> *It is not true that*
> *nice guys finish last;*
> *nice guys are winners*
> *before the game even starts.*
> —ADDISON WALKER

In any case, athletes don't have a monopoly on the competitive state of mind. Ultimately, competition is a state of mind that springs from comparing one's performance to someone else's. The competitive mind emerges in every aspect of life—between siblings, partners, men, and women. In such activities as modern dance, ballet, or painting, we find individuals who are jealously competitive. I've known professional athletes, on the other hand, who viewed their game as a cooperative "mutual-teaching session" between two teams. Steve Hug, one of the all-time best American gymnasts, never really competed *against* anyone, because he didn't have that kind of mentality. He simply did his best, measured by his own rather than anybody else's standards of excellence. Because of his approach, he was one of the most centered athletes and successful competitors I've known.

Even in "one-on-one" sports, such as basketball or football, it is possible, and often advantageous, to view one's opponents as teachers who serve you best by doing thier best. In the same way, you can best serve these comrades-in-sport by outperforming them. Once we view competition in this way, we do our best, but perhaps without the overtones of hostility and negativity that too often characterize the competitive psyche.

Winning and losing often depend upon circumstances that have little to do with relative prowess in a particular skill and may be circumstantial. I once won a world trampoline championship; I had a good day, but other athletes might have won on another day. To say that I was a superior trampolinist has little meaning—I "won" only that one competition. Fate, fortune, and a myriad of other factors have a lot to do with performance. So it seems wise not to take competition too seriously.

Free of the combative state of mind, we find no opponents—only people like ourselves, brothers and sisters in training, all striving toward excellence. Unfortunately, it appears that some of the more "successful" coaches view competition as if they were waging a holy war. Such intense rivalry probably does motivate some individuals and teams, but at what price to the mind and emotions?

The Moment of Truth itself, whether in performance or in the competitive arena, can serve as an exciting stimulus to excellence. Yet its purpose ends when the race ends. Once we catch a fish, we no longer need the net; when the competition is over, we need not linger over scores, numbers, or dead statistics. Yet colleges and professional teams preserve past scores like prize butterflies pressed into books. Many people become preoccupied with numbers, statistics, titles, victories.

Inner athletes have a way of forgetting the game's outcome the moment it is over, but they remember its lessons. Outer athletes learn few lasting lessons because they tend to get stuck on the outcomes.

Inner athletes can't afford to revel—or despair—over the past. Fame is fleeting, and glory fades. The only lasting value in the competitive experience are the lessons we learn and keep alive.

Ultimately, it makes no difference whether we praise or belittle competition. It exists, and it has a loyal following. If we do compete, we might as well give it our best shot, as we would any other aspect of life. But inner athletes maintain a cooperative, positive attitude toward all the players, even in the heat of competition.

In competition, theories of learning how to learn—and the laws of nature—may seem only vaguely relevant or interesting, and the gymnasium may seem the place for action rather than philosophy. But an expanded philosophy is going to inspire the athletes of the future.

Athletes can study biomechanical techniques for only so long; they can work only so hard; they can eat only so well. Eventually, it's going to be the more subtle elements of talent—those invisible qualities of mind and motivation—that will determine the master athletes. Work will always be a key element—in psychophysical work, imbued with the qualities of the inner athlete, that will make the difference. And if insight into the lessons of nature and the qualities of talent can help to develop a world champion, it can also help your game, no matter what your present level or experience.

> *If we don't invest much energy*
> *then defeat doesn't hurt as much*
> *but neither is winning very exciting.*
> —*DICK VERMEIL*

In the athlete arena we will always find those more and less skilled than ourselves. As we continue to progress, let's be careful not to become preoccupied with distant goals, or we may miss the pleasure of the climb. Whether our path on any given day is clear or rocky, the real and only measure of our achievement can be found in answer to a single question: *"Have I done my best today?"* All winning, losing, titles, and fame fall into the shadow of that question.

Overload-Cutback: Preparing for Competition

In the Moment of Truth, we focus our minds, emotions, and bodies on the game. Inner athletes can play as if their life depended upon their efforts, yet laugh at the outcome. Armed simultaneously with humor and intensity, they harness their fullest energies and potential.

Often in the heat of competition we transcend everyday limits. We have to be prepared for these bursts of adrenaline.

The primary tool many athletes and coaches use prior to competition is *overload and cutback*. As the name implies, the method is to overload the demand before competition, then cut back just before the day arrives.

The significance of this method is far more than physical; it also results in a psychological feeling of confidence, ease, and security. If you are about to run a five-mile race and you ran eight miles through the hills last week, you're not only going to be physically prepared, you're going to feel very relaxed and self-confident.

Although no coaches I've met have named this method, its use is almost universal. In gymnastics, for example, the athlete will overload on the number of repetitive routines, going as high as eighteen routines in a workout. After that, even if the athlete feels a little sluggish, the few routines he (or she) performs in a competition will seem easy.

Emphasize quantity as the season reaches a peak, then stress quality over quantity. The exact timing of the change in emphasis varies from sport to sport. The important thing is to build up to more than you'll be called upon to do in competition.

The following overload techniques can all be useful:

- Training with extra weight.

- Going greater distances or faster than necessary—or up hills.

- Practicing without the use of one sense—eyes closed,

for example—so that the other senses become more refined.

- Working under deliberately *poor conditions*. Jugglers, for example, may practice in dim light or windy conditions; ice skaters may train for a while on poor ice, in case they meet these conditions in competition; martial artists may practice their skills in the ocean surf or in a pool underwater.

- Increasing the normal demand. A baseball batter, for example, can have the pitcher throw fast balls from three-quarters the usual distance. If the batter can learn to hit those pitches, connecting with full-distance throws will be far easier.

How much overload you practice depends upon your own temperament, capacity, and activity. The main point of the exercise is to practice some kind of overload, then cut back for competition.

Emotional preparation

It's entirely normal, even desirable, to feel skittish, nervous, or anxious before a competition. Whether you experience the jitters as shaky knees, upset stomach, compulsive yawning, or other symptoms of "nerves," you'll want to know how to deal with pre-competition jitters.

Understanding the nature of the precompetitive body helps to overcome—and to use—the symptoms of nervousness. Remember that the competition is a ceremony, a special occasion when you are, in reality, tested. You *should* feel nervous! Your body is preparing for a unique demand: adrenaline is released into the bloodstream, stimulating a release of simple sugars into the muscles for extraordinary activity; your heart begins to beat faster; your breathing mechanisms are stimulated (thus the yawning). The muscles are trembling with readiness and energy.

Don't fight it! If you're just sitting there, waiting to start, you will feel shaky knees and stomach butterflies, because the body is ready to run, fight, jump, go . . . right now. If you feel these symptoms before you actually need them, you can control and use the flow of adrenaline by moving. Do some jumping jacks, run in place, or do a few push-ups. All the body's responses are designed to enable you to move faster, stronger, and better, so *move*.

If your mind is filled with negative images or ideas— "I'd better do well or it will be humiliating; my parents (girlfriend, boyfriend, teammates) are depending on me—I can't mess up; I hope I don't break my neck"—then you will experience the jitters as fear, weakness, or even paralysis.

If you work on positive images—"Now is my chance to come through in a real pinch; my parents (girlfriend, boyfriend, teammates) are going to be proud of me; wow, look at that enthusiastic audience"—then you'll experience these nerves as excitement and anticipation.

If you're predisposed to tense muscles, then the body's response to psyching up can be revved-up tension; if you've learned to relax, then you can channel and direct the extra energy.

Most of us *tend to perform in competition as we did in practice:* sometimes we'll be a little shaky, but usually we'll do a little better. Recognizing this, we can free ourselves of unrealistic expectations or fears. Results come in direct proportion to preparation.

The Mental Game

Competition tests all our capacities; physical skill is only one part of the game. It's not unusual for the most conditioned athletes to come in second or third because they haven't mastered the mental game. Physical experts can be weakened and distracted if they are susceptible to emotional flightiness or mental fuzziness. The ancient samurai warriors recognized that, if they were to reach old age, a razor-sharp mind and emotional calm must precede physical skill.

Experienced athletes usually fare well in high-pressure competitions. They're able to control their nervous energy; centered, they don't walk around gawking at the other athletes but focus on their own efforts; they've developed rhythms of warm-up and energy expenditure.

Experience comes from having learned the lessons of training. Some athletes gain a great deal of experience in a relatively short time. Other athletes may compete for years and never be seasoned because they haven't learned the right lessons.

Inner athletes *treat both training and competition with the same respect and intensity.* When they train, they apply the same mental focus and determination as if they were in competition; when they compete, they're as relaxed and easygoing as if they were practicing.

Competition is a test of our serenity and one-pointedness, a chance to show "grace under fire."

> *How we play the game*
> *reveals something of our character;*
> *how we lose*
> *shows all of it.*
>
> —*ANONYMOUS*

Your attitude in competition influences the attitudes of others. Psychological strategy can add a whole new dimension to competition and can turn a contest of brute strength and speed into a chess game. It requires mental acuity, refined judgment, and plain old intuition.

The only safe and sure way
to destroy your enemies
is to make them your friends.
　　　　—ANONYMOUS

Never get so involved in psychological strategy that you lose your own center and forget your primary objective: to present your own best effort, not to sabotage someone else's. It's not helpful to put someone mentally off-balance if, in the process, you fall off-balance too. The ultimate competitive strategy is to remain centered in your own unshakable confidence and calm, free of anyone else's influence. Still, appearing as a tower of strength and confidence can be incredibly distracting to the competition.

Above all, even as you play with your full determination and power, remember that the game will never be more than a game. The lessons it offers are important, but the game itself is only play. Every game makes *somebody* happy.

To inner athletes, every day is a learning experience; ultimately, *you can't lose.*

Although we've all heard or seen it, what better way to end this chapter than with a reminder from the Olympic Creed of 1894:

The most important thing is not to win,
but to take part,
just as the most important thing in life
is not the triumph,
but the attempt.
The essential thing is not to have conquered,
but to have fought well.

9 *New Frontiers:*
The Evolution of Athletics

**Unless we try to do something
beyond what we have already mastered,
we cannot grow.**

—RONALD OSBORN

Since ancient times, when leaping over bulls, fighting lions, and hitting rocks with a stick were the fashion, sports have come a long way. Never entirely static, sports evolve with the passing of time, reflecting the dominant, mainstream values of the culture in their rules, structure, creativity, and tolerance for violence.

Some sports, such as ice hockey, approach the traditions of the gladiators who often fought to the death for the entertainment of packed Roman stadiums. Other movement forms, such as gymnastics, sport acrobatics, diving, and ice skating, are evolving into performance arts, with all the elegance and aesthetics of the ballet.

It's wonderful that such a variety of sport forms exist to meet the interests and needs of different people.

The sports we choose to play, both as individuals and as a nation, warrant periodic scrutiny because they reflect our val-

148

ues as well as help shape and reinforce ways of acting and being that may have positive or negative carry-over in daily life.

Sports and games are fun. They're invigorating and boisterous; they encourage teamwork, timing, cooperation, and organization. Athletes are stronger and healthier in many ways than nonathletes. Everyone recognizes the benefits of running, jumping, swinging, swimming, throwing, catching, somersaulting, and balancing. At the same time, however, the growing intensity of competition can predispose the participants to chronic pains and injury, sometimes strengthening and at other times disabling.

Any influence so central to our lives, both physically and psychologically, must be approached with an attitude that is far more than casual. The benefits of training can far outweigh the liabilities. But instead of resting on that statement, let's see if there's a way to enhance the benefits of athletics further and to diminish the liabilities.

We can ask two important questions about any sport:

1. Does this sport contribute effectively to the physical and psychological well-being of the athlete?

2. Does this sport develop heightened capacity for daily life?

In light of these two questions, we can assess the relative social value of a particular sport (beyond its entertainment value) to see if some changes in that sport might be in order.

The broken records of each new Olympic Games reflect new heights of achievement. Yet, from the psychophysical perspective, training is still at a rudimentary level. If we look at the realities of high-pressure competitive sport today, we can see many examples of a "moving violation" of the natural laws of balance.

Many favorite pastimes, including such games as tennis, bowling, golf, and baseball, create imbalances in the natural symmetry of the body. It's not that we should abandon such activities, but we can balance these liabilities by wise training.

Even with all the new techniques of scientific measurement and systematic methods of physical development, our approach to athletic training is still evolving. We've only begun to appreciate and reap the potential benefits of athletics.

But we are seeing the birth of a new tradition, one in which sports are consciously designed for overall well-being; eventually, I believe, we will replace the worn-out or outdated games of the past with the new and revamped sports that will suit the future better.

The most obvious way of changing sports is through modifications of the rules.

Changing the Rules. The rules of today's sports have developed over long periods of time. They're reflections of our views of what is fair and just and right; they indicate the current state of our wavering tolerance for violence and our striving for beauty and spirit. Any changes in rules must therefore be undertaken with the greatest care.

At this point I want to suggest one basic rule change that would render some of our most popular games more interesting, more challenging, and far healthier for our bodies:

Symmetrical Training

Golf, tennis, bowling, baseball, and many other sports that make primary use of one side of the body are marvelous games. They are, however, debilitating to the symmetry of the body, and symmetry is vital for our natural alignment to earth's gravitational pull. By a simple rule change we can increase the value of these games and eliminate their major liability: We can require these athletes to make equal use of both arms.

There are several arguments against such a rule change: First, equipment modifications would, in many cases, be necessary. Second, the stars of today would have to make some fast adjustments in order to remain stars. Third, those of us who were just beginning to feel proficient would have to undergo a temporary "klutzy" period again.

Now let's look at the benefits of *symmetrical training*:

- Chronic pains of elbow, back, or shoulder would be lessened or eliminated by working both sides of the body, since each side would be given a periodic rest.

- You could practice more without fatigue.

- You would in many situations be more versatile, thereby spicing up your game.

- You would eliminate the sport's postural imbalances, resulting in freedom from one-sided tension in the arm, shoulder, and along the spinal cord, and you would attain better alignment in gravity.

- If you were getting a little stale, this new challenge would be guaranteed to bring you to life.

- You may become a better performer because some research shows that learning a skill on one side increases learning facility on the other, and can, in fact, help eliminate old weak habits.

The rule of symmetry, if applied to our one-sided sports and games, would benefit health and well-being. This new rule would be fundamentally aligned with the natural laws. (Although clearly beneficial, the change hasn't happened so far because of reluctance by the participants and clinging to the status quo.) The second and most important way we can personally influence the evolution of sport is by altering our own approach.

Re-Visioning Sports

Casey Cook, diver and inspirational athlete I coached at Oberlin College, told me that the sport of diving evolved for him as he began to view his movements in terms of energy awareness. He felt as if he were "sculpting" energy as he somer-saulted his way into the air, forming lines of energy he could almost see. As he learned to shape the direction of energy flow, he felt he was playing a new game—on "nature's team," with the board, the air, and the water as teammates. He was no longer a lonely body, bouncing on a board, mechanically spin-ning, attempting to knife through the water for a judge's reward. During leisure hours, if he played baseball or threw a Frisbee, he still enjoyed this sense of energy flow and graceful harmony with the natural forces. Without a single rule change, Casey had "changed" the sport of diving, at least for himself.

Professional football player Chip Oliver quit the profes-sional ranks at the height of his career because he realized that the sport as *he had played it* was not good for the body or the spirit. After studying yoga and other integrative disciplines, Chip came to realize that for him, football "hurt too much." Later, Chip was drawn back into the sport he loved, but with a new approach to the game—using football as a means to blend with others, to practice symmetry, to master relaxation-in-move-ment, and to use the sport as a lesson in living.

No single sport has appeal for everyone. No matter what our chosen form of athletic expression, for inner athletes it embodies universal qualities that can enhance anyone's game and amplify its benefits:

Mental
- Encourages attitude of blending and harmonizing rather than collision; it presupposes no "opponents" or "enemies," just teachers.

- Enhances ability to "see" the flow of energy.

- Demands and develops one-pointed concentration.

Emotional
- Encourages friendly, cooperative interaction.

- Contains sufficient pressure or risk to challenge the participant to higher levels of courage, balance, and "grace under pressure."

- Serves as a laboratory to understand yourself and others.

- Creates an atmosphere of mutual help and support through teamwork.

Physical
- Balances development of the body.

- Develops sensitivity to the body's needs instead of encouraging the ignoring of pain signals.

- Demands (and develops) suppleness of all body joints.

- Develops cardiovascular fitness and whole-body stamina.

- Aids muscular symmetry and postural alignment in gravity, placing stress factors on both sides.

- Enhances the body's connection to the earth through dynamic calm and relaxation-in-movement.

Many of the preceding attributes may not automatically be part of everyone's game, but if inner athletes notice an important aspect lacking—and there are weak elements in every sport—they find compensatory activities to balance their game. A football player, for example, might take up T'ai Chi; an ice-hockey ace might practice hatha yoga; a baseball player might practice ballet; a yogi might take up karate.

Most of us find ourselves involved in a particular sport, game, or movement activity as a result of a variety of influences, including the views of parents, early exposure, or something we saw on television. It seems critical for any young person with generally good coordination to sample many sports and movement activities, not just those the parents happen to approve of. I've seen potential swimming champions pushed into football or other sports because of parental interest. If youngsters get a broad exposure to a variety of sports and games, including dance, martial arts, and other activities, they will naturally gravitate to the form that works best for them.

For those of you who wonder what the *perfect* game is for them, however, I suggest that it doesn't exist. Just like people, each game has its strong and weak points; different benefits and liabilities. Gymnastics, for example, offers impressive development of a wide array of physical qualities, but lacks the relaxed, socializing team interraction of baseball—which fails to offer the variety of physical qualities. And so it goes.

The main thing for inner athletes to keep in mind is to choose the game that fits one's individual physical and psychological needs. When I discovered the trampoline and then the other gymnastics events, I knew this activity was for me; I didn't have to analyze it, I felt it. The degree of satisfaction and challenge, or just plain fun, available in any athletic activity are all good measures of whether you've found your match.

Games of the Masters

If the peak cannot be reached
without losing touch with the body,
or if it is reached
through alienation of the body,
then new games must be invented.
    —DR. MICHAEL CONANT

Inner athletes do not care for victory at all costs. They recognize that ultimate victory means personal growth and long-range, lifetime benefits. So they naturally gravitate to new and experimental forms of exploration and fun. I end this section with a preview of sports to come, a vision of tomorrow, a sampling of some "new" sports. They by no means exhaust the possibilities.

—————— SLOW-MOTION RUNNING ——————
A New Approach

Object: To finish the race *last.*

Rules:
1. Competitors begin on the starting line, facing the finish (a wall) 10 yards away.

2. At the signal "Go!" all runners must begin to move continuously—without stopping their forward motion—in a direct line toward the finish.

3. Each step must be a length of at least 12 inches (measure by 9 parallel lines, drawn between the starting line and finish).

Discussion. Slow-motion running is a far more challenging sport than may appear at a glance. In trying to reach the wall last, the best athlete will have to move with awesome slowness. This requires excellent balance, sensitivity, the ability to relax, and a kind of dynamic patience. The ability to perform in this way reflects an entirely new kind of psychophysical stamina, a quality of body-mind balance rarely explored in usual sports. Slow-motion running is a form of moving meditation similar to that practiced by practitioners of Zen meditation. If you try it sometime, you'll appreciate its challenging nature and meditative repose. It's a perfect balance to the speedy pace of most of today's athletics.

THE NEW GYMNASTICS
Efficiency and Fun

Object: As in other gymnastics events—to score as close as possible to a perfect 10 on every event, through sufficient endurance and skill, flawless technique, and aesthetic style and presentation.

Rules:

1. Men's and women's events have been combined, so that men and women can compete with one another on an equal basis. This is possible with the new events because in gymnastics, athletes handle only their own body weight.

2. There are four events:

Floor-beam exercise. A combination of floor exercise and beam. A padded beam, 5 inches wide, adjustable between 2½ and 3½ feet high, is placed along the inside border of the padded, resilient floor-exercise area.

Each athlete performs a 2-minute routine to musical accompaniment. In addition to the regular tumbling, dance, and floor-exercise work, the gymnast must travel the complete length of the beam 3 times, with turns, balance, and aerial elements, including a flowing mount and dismount for each passage.

Trampoline. A net-like bouncing surface allows any performer to achieve sufficient height. The trampoline is completely padded all around with a 6-foot border of 8-inch-thick pads, and springs are covered.

The performers engage in 15 bounces total, judged on the basis of difficulty height, form, and control.

Double horizontal bar. The gymnast performs a horizontal-bar routine, but is required to pass through the air from one bar to the other at least 3 times during the routine. There is safety padding beneath the bars.

Sport acrobatics. Each team shows 6 routines of aesthetic pair work. 3 routines consist of pairs of the same sex (may be male-male, or female-female), and 3 routine are mixed pairs. Each routine is done in harmony with suitable music. Each routine must show balance, tumbling, dance, strength, all in tempo and in harmony with one's partner.

Discussion. The new gymnastics offers a combination of mental and physical demands found in few other sports—an optimal combination of events to give the body balanced development. (All four events are universal spectator favorites.) The four events consolidate all the primary benefits of gymnastics (strength, suppleness, stamina, and sensitivity—particularly, a refined kinesthetic sense). Men and women would be afforded the uncommon social opportunity to train together, as equals. With less apparatus to buy, more programs could be set up around the country.

T'AI CHI-DO
The Power of Synthesis

Object: Using slow motion to refine the movements of any practice— in this case, Aikido.

Rules: None (noncompetitive)

T'ai Chi-do incorporates the refined, slow motion training of T'ai Chi with the flowing, energy-blending qualities of Aikido.

T'ai chi, which originated in China, uses, at beginning levels, slow-motion, softness, and sensitivity.

Aikido is entirely nonviolent in intent—never designed to injure another deliberately—and emphasizes positive energy flow through relaxed movement to deflect, channel, and control an attacker's energy through the use of graceful throws and wrist locks. Aikido contains a lighthearted blending of movement and energy and practice in falling and smooth rolling (not included in t'ai chi).

When we think of self-defense, we usually imagine defense from a human attacker. This imagery is limited. Through the practice of T'ai Chi or Aikido, one learns how to blend with everyday problems and stresses, from tension, fatigue, and lowered resistance (which attack us far more than human adversaries do). Aikido rolls are especially useful to people who may have occasion to fall and want to do it smoothly and creatively.

In the same manner we can combine slow motion elements of T'ai Chi with another martial art, we can combine the positive qualities of other practices.

EFFORTLESS TENNIS
From Competition to Cooperation

Object: To keep the ball in play as long as possible, becoming a teacher rather than an opponent to the person(s) across the net.

Rules: May be played as singles or doubles; the

idea is to hit the ball so that the other players can return it while stretching their own abilities.

Discussion: Originated by Brent Zeller, San Francisco Bay Area tennis coach, this approach to tennis is played in the spirit of mutual support rather than as two mock "enemies" each trying to get the other person to fail. Among its advantages:

- A better, longer-lasting aerobic workout, since volleys tend to be a lot longer.

- Faster improvement, because it involves more time actually moving and hitting the ball, as a result of longer volleys.

- Less stress; players maintain more relaxed bodies.

- More fun.

- Players of all different skill levels and experience can play with one another because the game challenges beginners and experts equally.

—————— THUNDERBALL ——————
A Non-Contact Martial Art

Object: Applying all principles of centeredness, balance, breathing, relaxation, and body/mind coordination inherent in martial arts, particularly T'ai Chi. Partners pass one, two, three, four, five, or even six balls back and forth in a flowing fashion, without getting hit.

Rules: An entirely cooperative practice, with the following guidelines:

---

1. Breathe profoundly and consciously.

2. Avoid getting hit! (After all, it is a martial art.)

3. Let go and flow. (Do not grab; yield, offer no resistance).

4. Stay aligned and allied with gravity (no awkward bending).

5. Train both sides of the body.

6. Cooperate with your partner.

Discussion: Originated by Robert David Morningstar, a gifted T'ai Chi teacher in New York City, this fast-growing movement form is perhaps one of the most enjoyable ever created—enjoyable in the sense that it produces a state of mental clarity and stillness from the first few minutes of play.

Challenging at every level, from beginner through mastery whether played with one partner or more, it differs from juggling in that participants do not catch and throw balls but rather return them without grasping, in a circular motion, using martial arts principles. Advanced practitioners have been known to handle as many as six balls at once! This art has to be seen to be appreciated and practiced to be enjoyed.

The uses and designs of sport are limitless. Since athletics is a mirror of daily life, you can bend your creative energies toward improving and evolving the benefits of conscious movement forms.

Athletics can be a means of enjoyment, recreation, psycho-fitness, biofeedback or, as you will increasingly discover, a way of transcendence, of unity—a path to a spiritual life. The door is open. We have only to walk through.

Epilogue:
Mastery of the Moving Experience

**If one advances confidently
in the direction of his dreams,
and endeavors to live the life which he has imagined,
he will meet with a success
unexpected in common hours.**

—HENRY DAVID THOREAU

Los Angeles, 1952. A new house was under construction on Redcliff Street. Up on the roof, atop the rafters, twenty feet above the street, stood a small boy, about to jump, staring down at a sand pile below, balancing precariously. I remember it well; that six-year-old boy was me.

Below, looking up, stood Steve Yusa, a boyhood friend and mentor—older, wiser, and (it seemed) far braver than I was. He was, in my eyes, a supreme warrior; afraid of nothing, he met every challenge. With a shout, he would leap from that rooftop like the Vikings I had seen in the movies, leaping with sword in hand down to the wolves.

Now it was my turn to jump, and my knees had turned to pudding.

"Come on, Danny, you can do it."

"I don't know. . .." I wanted to jump but stood there,

161

trembling, for the better part of what seemed like an hour.

"Come on, do it!" Steve repeated. But I couldn't budge. Until Steve said something that changed my life: "Danny. *Stop thinking and jump!*" The next thing I knew I was soaring into space.

Twelve years later, in 1964, at the World Trampoline Championships in London, I rubbed the jet lag and two hour's sleep from my eighteen year-old eyes and opened the door to the arena. Surveying the colorful scene, I saw nearly thirty trampoline champions from their respective countries, warming up, bouncing blurs of blue and yellow, red and green and gold, rocketing up, soaring skyward, somersaulting and twisting through the air. In about four hours, one of us would be champion of the world.

In the end it came down to Gary Erwin, reigning NCAA champion, and me. I watched Gary's final routine; it looked flawless. I was going to have to pull out all the stops.

My legs felt a little numb and shaky as I started bouncing, higher and higher, preparing to explode into a twisting double somersault and begin my final routine. I experienced a flash of doubt; then, from a near-forgotten rooftop, a voice echoed from the past: Stop thinking and jump! I stopped thinking and soared into space—to the championship of the world.

April, 1968. I joined my teammates in our quest to win our first National Collegiate Gymnastics Championships. The competition was one of the closest in NCAA history. In the end, it was all up to me, the last performer. My coach and teammates sat holding their breath and biting their lips as I chalked my hands and leaped to the horizontal bar.

The crowd was so hushed that the sound of my chalked hands sliding around the bar seemed the only sound in the arena; I knew that my teammates were going around the bar with me in their hearts and minds.

"Come on, Dan, you can do it . . . stop thinking, stop thinking. . . ."

A power beyond physical strength surged through me; beyond fear or doubt, with total focus and determination, I leapt to the bar. I found myself performing a movement I had never done in competition before. Then, time stood still as I released the bar and flew upward, floating in the zone, somersaulting, seeing the ceiling, the floor, the ceiling. . . .

Everything depended on the landing; it had to be perfect. My body stretched open, dropping toward the mats. In the next instant I knew—even before I heard the roar of the crowd, before my coach grabbed and shook my hand: I had done it. Yet "I" had done nothing. There was only that experience of everything happening, as if on its own—a moment bigger than I was, larger than life.

I would never be the same again. I had experienced a Whole greater than the sum of its parts; my life would become simpler and, at the same time, more interesting.

I began to see that problems I encountered in sport or daily life resulted more from disharmony between by body, mind, and emotions than from my external circumstances. I knew that life would always have its challenges, but as I created deeper levels of internal integration and balance, my perceptions changed and I began to respond to those challenges in more constructive ways. Where before I saw stumbling blocks, I now saw steppingstones; my problems become opportunities, and every difficulty became a form of "spiritual weightlifting"—a means to strengthen my spirit.

Those mystic moments in which we "see" lines of energy, feel what other players are going to do before they do it, or experience a oneness with others in the arena remind us that there is more to life, and more to ourselves, than we had once imagined.

It doesn't matter what we call those special moments—satori, "the zone," or "a peak experience"—they provide a preview of our highest potential. As our field of training opens up and reveals its secrets, its hidden potential, it becomes a vehicle for personal mastery.

Today, more than ever, many athletes report extraordinary experiences ranging from paranormal abilities and perceptions to moments of unreasonable happiness, independent of whether they win or lose. Time slows down or even stands still, yet hours may race by like minutes. In these special moments they feel a dazzling sensory clarity or a sense of being fully alive. Such peak experiences inspire us and call us to the ultimate truth of the athletic experience: that the varied forms of movement training are, as Bruce Lee once reminded us, "different fingers pointing at the moon; if we focus on the finger, we miss the moon's glory." We train on different paths, but we climb the same mountain of self-mastery.

The inner athlete's journey is a hero's journey, one in which victories are measured not by times or scores but by our progress on this larger quest. Training is a secret school, a mystery school, the Way of the Inner Athlete. Spectators can watch and cheer; philosophers can ruminate about the trials and glories; but only those who have tasted it, who have reached out, leapt, danced, stretched, and sweated for it, know its sweetness and its promise. The spirit of the athlete was perhaps best expressed in the words of Theodore Roosevelt, who said:

> *It is not the critic who counts;*
> *not the one who points out*
> *how the strong stumbled,*
> *or where the doer of deeds*
> *could have done better.*
> *The credit belongs to those*
> *in the arena;*
> *who strive valiantly;*
> *who fail and come up short*
> *again and again;*
> *who know great enthusiasm*
> *and great devotion;*
> *who at the best*
> *know in the end the triumph*

of high achievement;
and who, at the worst,
if they fail, at least fail while
daring greatly,
so that their place shall never be
with those timid souls
who know neither victory nor defeat.

The university remains the domain of the intellect; the temple is the domain of the heart; the gymnasium is the arena of vitality. We each have the university, the temple, and the gymnasium within us. We humans stand at the last frontier, the inward journey, as we discover the laws of the universe within our own bodies—the journey of the inner athlete, realizing our fullest potential. The reward is commensurate with the effort.

It is moving within
a multitude of sensations and forces
effortlessly, fluidly,
without a trace of
inappropriate exertion or tension.
It is being danced by God at each moment,
pirouetting, leaping, eluding all forces
that work to trip up and snare the Dancer.
                              —*ROBIN CARLSEN*

The journey of the inner athlete is the journey of humanity, mirrored in many ways—a riddle few have solved or have even seen.

Training is the path and the process, the means and end, a bridge to personal evolution.

As a World Culture, we are passing through the bittersweet lessons of material wealth and abject poverty, of excess and hunger, of technical knowledge not yet tempered by wisdom; no longer satisfied with symbolic solutions, we are seeking world peace and inner peace, a goal waiting because it is beyond the intellect, found only when the heart is open and body and mind are in balance. In that balance are the secret teachings of this world.

The map is complete: We see that the laws of nature, the laws of athletics, and the laws of living are one and the same. There is no escaping from these laws; we are both bound by them and liberated by them. The way of the inner athlete is the way of balance—discipline without extremes; loving in principle and in action, when we would tend to withdraw from love; being happy whether or not we have a good reason.

Rebirth of the Master Athlete

Many of the athletes we see on television have reached a high level of physical fitness; but many have not yet realized their potential as inner athletes. At the Olympics, at Wimbleton, or at Pebble Beach, we may see many experts but relatively few masters. The following story illustrates the difference:

> *One day in feudal Japan, a master of the tea ceremony was on an errand in the marketplace and collided with a foul-tempered samurai. Immediately, the swordsman demanded an apology for the "insult" in the form of a duel to the death.*
>
> *The tea master was in no position to decline, though he had no expertise with swords. He asked if he could complete his obligations for the day before meeting the samurai for the duel. It was agreed that they'd meet in a nearby orchard, later in the afternoon.*
>
> *His errands completed early, the tea master stopped to visit the house of Miyamoto Musashi, a famous swordmaster and painter. The tea master told Master Miyamoto his situation and asked if the swordmaster could teach him*

how to behave so as to die honorably.

"That is an unusual request," replied Miyamoto, "but I'll help if I can." Detecting an air of composure about the small man standing before him, Miyamoto asked him what art he practised.

"I serve tea," he replied.

"Excellent! Then serve me tea," said Miyamoto.

Without hesitation, the tea master took his utensils from a pouch and began, with the utmost serenity and concentration, to perform the graceful, meditative ceremony of preparing, serving, and appreciating o-cha, the green tea.

Miyamoto was impressed by this man's obvious composure on the afternoon of his death. The tea master was apparently free of all thought about his fate waiting a few hours hence. Ignoring any thoughts of fear, he focused his attention upon the present moment of beauty.

"You already know how to die well," said Miyamoto, "but you can do this. . . . " Then Miyamoto instructed him how to die honorably, ending with "it will probably end in a mutual slaying."

The tea master bowed and thanked the swordmaster. Carefully, he wrapped his implements and left for the duel.

He saw the swordsman waiting impatiently, anxious to get this petty killing over. The tea master approached the samurai, laid his implements down as gently as he would a tiny infant—as if he expected to pick them up again in a few moments. Then, as Miyamoto had suggested, he bowed graciously to the samurai, as calmly as if he were about to serve him tea. Next, he raised his sword with but a single thought in his mind—to strike the samurai, no matter what.

As he stood, sword raised, mind focused, he saw the sword expert's eyes grow wide with wonder, then perplexity, then respect, then fear. No longer did the swordsman see a meek little man before him; now he saw

a fearless warrior, an invincible opponent who had mas-
tered the fear of death. Raised over the tea master's head,
glinting blood-red in the sun's last rays, the samurai saw
his own death.

The sword expert hesitated for a moment, then low-
ered his sword—and his head. He begged to apologize to
this little tea master, who later became his teacher in the
art of living without fear.

Leaving the bushes from where he had concealed him-
self, Miyamoto stretched with pleasure, yawning like a
cat. Grinning, he scratched his neck, turned, and walked
home to a hot bath, a bowl of rice, and sleep without
dreams.

Masters of one art have mastered the inner principles of
all arts because they have mastered themselves. With
dominion over both mind and muscle, they demonstrate
power, serenity, and spirit. They not only have talent for
sport, they have an expanded capacity for life. The experts
shine in the competitive arena; the masters shine everywhere.

For the inner athlete, physical skill is only a byproduct of
internal development.

Master athletes may remain unnoticed by those around
them because their internal skills are visible only to those who
understand. Because they do everything naturally, they don't
stand out. When observing them closely, we see a certain relaxation, an effortless quality, and a kind of peaceful humor. They
have no need to play a holy role or to act "together." They have
seen their lives upside down and inside out and have nothing
left to defend or to prove.

Whatever they do, they practice; whatever they practice
receives their undivided attention. They radiate security; others follow, although the masters have no particular desire to
lead. When they wash dishes, they only wash dishes; their
minds become washcloths. When they walk, their minds are

walking with them; when they cook, their minds are food on the grill; when they sweep, their minds clean the world.

> *The body moves naturally, automatically, without any personal intervention or awareness. If we think too much, our actions become slow and hesitant. When questions arise, the mind tires; consciousness flickers and wavers like a candle flame in a breeze.*
>
> —*TAISEN DESHIMARU*

Master athletes view life as their practice, and they create a ceremony out of every moment. They fold clothes, eat, wash their faces, stand or sit down with the same attention we might give to a championship game. Their decisions have a three-dimensional quality, balanced among rationality, intuition, and gut instinct. Their decisions therefore always end up "right," natural, and appropriate. Ordinary, yet full of energy, force, and quality, they reveal the spirit of a peaceful warrior.

Masters serve as reminders that all specific practices are subordinate to the practice of life. Use natural law to master athletics; use athletics to master natural law.

Imagine yourself approaching the top of a mountain, feeling a growing internal alignment with the rhythms of nature. In the flow, the zone, the state of satori, you round the last bend in the path and see the peak before you. Then you notice someone standing there, smiling at you with bright, clear eyes—a master of daily life. You walk right up to the master, filled with gratitude. As the master's face comes into focus, and you realize that the master is you.

END

About the Author

 Dan Millman is the author of *Way of the Peaceful Warrior* and other inspiring books for adults and children. His writings, which distill universal wisdom and a variety of mind-body disciplines, have been translated into fourteen languages. A former world champion athlete, coach, and college professor, he currently writes, lectures, and trains those interested in the field of personal growth.

To Contact Dan Millman

For a brochure of tapes and trainings, call or or write:
Peaceful Warrior Services
Box 6148, San Rafael, CA 94903
Phone (415) 491-0301
Fax (415) 491-0856